James Madison and the Spirit of Republican Self-Government

In the first study that combines an in-depth examination of James Madison's *National Gazette* essays of 1791–92 with a study of *The Federalist*, Colleen A. Sheehan traces the evolution of Madison's conception of the politics of communication and public opinion throughout the Founding period, demonstrating how "the sovereign public" would form and rule in America.

Contrary to those scholars who claim that Madison dispensed with the need to form an active and virtuous citizenry, Sheehan argues that Madison's vision for the new nation was informed by the idea of republican self-government, whose manifestation he sought to bring about in the spirit and way of life of the American people. Madison's story is "the story of an idea" – the idea of America.

Colleen A. Sheehan is Professor of Political Science at Villanova University and has served in the Pennsylvania House of Representatives. She is the coeditor of *Friends of the Constitution: Writings of the Other Federalists, 1787–1788*, and author of numerous articles on the American Founding and eighteenth-century political and moral thought; these have appeared in journals such as the *William and Mary Quarterly*, *American Political Science Review*, *Review of Politics*, and *Persuasions: The Jane Austen Journal*.

For Jack

James Madison and the Spirit of Republican Self-Government

COLLEEN A. SHEEHAN
Villanova University

CAMBRIDGE
UNIVERSITY PRESS

CAMBRIDGE UNIVERSITY PRESS
Cambridge, New York, Melbourne, Madrid, Cape Town, Singapore, São Paulo, Delhi

Cambridge University Press
32 Avenue of the Americas, New York, NY 10013-2473, USA

www.cambridge.org
Information on this title: www.cambridge.org/9780521727334

First published 2009

Printed in the United States of America

A catalog record for this publication is available from the British Library.

Library of Congress Cataloging in Publication Data

Sheehan, Colleen A.
James Madison and the spirit of republican self-government / Colleen A. Sheehan.
  p.   cm.
Includes bibliographical references and index.
ISBN 978-0-521-89874-4 (hardback) – ISBN 978-0-521-72733-4 (pbk.)
1. Madison, James, 1751–1836 – Political and social views.   2. United States – Politics and
government – 1783–1809.   3. United States – Politics and government – Philosophy.
4. Republicanism – United States – History – 18th century.   5. Representative government
and representation – United States – History – 18th century.   6. Democracy – United States –
History – 18th century.   7. Communication – Political aspects – United States – History –
18th century. 8. Public opinion – Political aspects – United States – History – 18th century.
9. Political science – United States – History – 18th century.   I. Title.
E342.S53   2009
973.5'1092–dc22   2008008946

ISBN   978-0-521-89874-4 hardback
ISBN   978-0-521-72733-4 paperback

Contents

Acknowledgments

This book has been a long time in the making, and I have incurred a great many debts along the way to its completion. The Earhart Foundation, the James Madison Program in American Ideals and Institutions of Princeton University, the National Endowment for the Humanities, and Villanova University generously supported various stages of my research. I particularly wish to thank David Kennedy, Ingrid A. Gregg, Robby George, Bruce Cole, and Michael Poliakoff for their encouragement and support of this project.

Bente Polites, Special Collections Librarian of the Falvey Memorial Library of Villanova University, was critical to the progress of this book. Only with Bente's advice and assistance was I able to advance my research on French Enlightenment thinkers, especially Jacques Peuchet and Jean Jacques Barthélemy. I am also grateful to Andrew Bausch, Laura Butterfield, and Clyde Ray for their able research assistance, and to Douglas Rice and Luke Perez for their kind help in proofreading the manuscript.

John Doody, Lance Banning, William Allen, Michael McGiffert, Henry Olsen, Michael Fiore, Michelle Gorman, Wight Martindale, and Darren Staloff read portions of the manuscript and kindly offered recommendations for improvement. I am especially grateful to Alan Gibson, Ralph Lerner, and Paul Rahe, who reviewed the entire manuscript and offered many perceptive and immensely helpful comments and suggestions. I am deeply appreciative of the time they so generously gave and the knowledge they freely shared to make this a better work.

Over the many years that I have studied the American Founding, I owe the most to two scholars and friends: William B. Allen and Lance Banning. While Bill Allen did not introduce me to the study of the early Republic, he is a large part of the reason that I continued to pursue my interest in Madison and the American Founding so many years ago. Bill is an excellent scholar and a superb teacher and mentor; our conversations over the years are really one conversation, for each time we talk we seem simply to pick up from where we left off, as if no time had elapsed. My debt to him is ongoing, and it is one that, try as I might, I am not able to repay.

Because of our mutual interest in the American Founding and especially in Madison, Lance Banning and I became colleagues and ultimately good friends. His work on Madison is unrivaled among scholars and will continue indefinitely to influence the way we understand the man from Montpelier. Since he cared more about advancing a sound understanding of Madison and the American Founding than he did about the accolades he personally deserved, Lance took the time to converse with me and other more junior scholars and unselfishly supported our work. Two years ago the still-young Lance Banning passed away unexpectedly, and we are poorer now that he is gone. Lance's legacy lives on, however, not only in the first-rate scholarship he left behind but also in the genuine community of interdisciplinary scholars on the Founding that he contributed so much to creating.

This book draws freely from some articles and essays that have appeared in somewhat different form in earlier publications. A small portion of Chapter 1 is based on "Madison's Party Press Essays," *Interpretation: A Journal in Political Philosophy* 7:3 (1990), 355–77. Portions of Chapters 2, 4, 5, and the Epilogue draw from "Madison v. Hamilton: The Battle over Republicanism and the Role of Public Opinion," originally published in the *American Political Science Review* 98:3 (2004), 405–24, and subsequently published in Douglas Ambrose and Robert W. T. Martin, eds., *The Many Faces of Alexander Hamilton: The Life and Legacy of America's Most Elusive Founding Father* (New York: New York University Press, 2006), 165–208. Chapter 3 is based largely on "Madison and the French Enlightenment: The Authority of Public Opinion," *William and Mary Quarterly* 49:3 (2002), 925–56. "The Commerce of Ideas and Cultivation of Character in Madison's Republic," in Bradley C. Watson, ed., *Civic Education and Culture* (Wilmington, Del.: ISI Books, 2006), 49–72, served as a preliminary draft for Chapter 4; parts of this essay are also blended into Chapters 1 and the Epilogue. A portion of Chapter 7 is taken from "The Politics of Public Opinion: James Madison's 'Notes on Government,'" *William and Mary Quarterly* 49:3 (1992), 609–27. I am grateful to the publishers of these journals and books for allowing me to reprint this material.

Throughout this undertaking, the constant support I have received from my family and friends has meant much to me. My best friend, Jack Doody, has been by my side through the thick and thin of this scholarly endeavor. He put up with me for all the times that we had to say "no" to a kind invitation because I was working on "Madison." I am fortunate to have as my husband a scholar and a critic who encourages me in my work and who is not satisfied unless I am. He has willingly devoted endless hours to our conversations on the Founding, most of them marked by patience and all of them by a great deal of cheerful encouragement. To him I dedicate this book.

Abbreviations for Sources

CSW   Condorcet, Marie Jean Antoine Nicolas de Caritat. *Selected Writings*. Edited by Keith Michael Baker. Indianapolis: Bobbs-Merrill, 1976.

Federalist   Hamilton, Alexander, James Madison, and John Jay. *The Federalist Papers*. Edited by Clinton Rossiter. Introduction and notes by Charles R. Kesler. New York: Mentor Books, [1788] 1999.

PAH   Syrett, Harold C. and Jacob E. Cooke, eds. *The Papers of Alexander Hamilton*, 26 vols. New York: Columbia University Press, 1961–79.

PJM   Hutchinson, William T. et al., eds. *The Papers of James Madison*. Chicago and Charlottesville: University of Chicago Press and University Press of Virginia, 1962–.

PTJ   Boyd, Julian P. et al., eds. *The Papers of Thomas Jefferson*. Princeton, N.J.: Princeton University Press, 1950–.

SOL   Montesquieu, Charles-Louis de Secondat, Baron de La Brède et de. *The Spirit of the Laws*. Translated and edited by Anne M. Cohler, Basia Carolyn Miller, and Harold Samuel Stone. Cambridge: Cambridge University Press, 1989.

Voyage   Barthélemy, Jean Jacques. *Voyage du jeune Anacharsis en Grèce dans le Milieu du Quatrième Siècle avant l'ère vulgaire*, 8 vols. Paris, 1788. The English translation used herein is Jean Jacques Barthélemy. *Travels of Anacharsis the Younger in Greece during the Middle of the Fourth Century before the Christian Aera*, 4th ed., 8 vols. London, 1806.

WJA   Adams, Charles Francis, ed. *The Works of John Adams*, 6
        vols. Freeport, N.Y.: Books for Libraries Press, 1850–56.
WJM   Hunt, Gaillard, ed. *The Writings of James Madison*, 9 vols.
        New York: G. P. Putnam's Sons, 1900–10.
WTJ   Lipscomb, Andrew A. and Albert Ellery Bergh, eds. *The
        Writings of Thomas Jefferson*, Memorial edition, 20 vols.
        Washington, D.C.: The Thomas Jefferson Memorial Asso-
        ciation, 1903–4.

Preface

About two years ago I was flying from Burlington, Vermont, to the Midwest. Across the aisle an older gentleman in jeans and a crisp plaid shirt, with weathered skin and hands not afraid of hard work, slowly turned the pages of a thick tome that rested on his lap. When we landed and stood to collect our belongings, I saw that the book he had been reading was David McCullough's *John Adams*. When I asked what he thought of it, he told me that he found it to be a fascinating account of a man and an age he previously hadn't known a lot about. He mentioned that he found in the character of John Adams a man worth getting to know. I nodded ever so slightly and returned the gentle, friendly smile of, I supposed, a New England farmer as we turned to exit the plane and go our separate ways.

At the time, I was working night and day on the manuscript that would become this book. My goal then, as now, was to come to know Madison as well as I could and to try to convey that understanding to others. I realized then that I also hoped one day a New England farmer would read my book and remark that James Madison was a man worth getting to know. The difficulty was that I was not writing a biography but a work of political theory, which does not easily make for a good story, unless, of course, one is as talented as Plato, which I certainly am not. Another stiff challenge, even for the biographer, is that Madison was a quiet, reserved man whose life was not, like Alexander Hamilton's, for example, "so tumultuous" and "stuffed with high drama . . . that only an audacious novelist could have dreamed it up."[1] Madison was not born a bastard son of a Scotch peddler on a remote Caribbean island, nor was he mortally wounded in a duel of honor in the prime of his life. He was not brazen or impetuous or dashing. He had no

[1] Ron Chernow, *Alexander Hamilton* (New York: Penguin Books, 2004), 4.

love affair that would threaten public disgrace, in the face of which he would stand tall and accept full responsibility.

Madison was an unimposing and somewhat frail fellow who often had to be asked to speak up so that he could be heard. His sense of himself was marked by a plain solidity rather than the pained puritanical labors of John Adams or the Continental ease of Thomas Jefferson. He was neither condescending nor competitive for fame, but content to leave the glory to others, or better yet, to America.[2] Although he left behind a prolific set of writings, his correspondence was not crafted to be an open window upon his life and character. He did little if anything to construct a myth of himself for history.

In sum, Madison's modesty, steadiness of character, and scholarly habits do not lend themselves to the storyteller's penchant to display the eccentric and colorfully vivid moments of the human persona and drama. This is not to say, however, that Madison lacked passion or spiritedness. His relationships with his dearest friends, whether William Bradford in his college days or Thomas Jefferson throughout his life, show that it would be a grave mistake to dismiss him as a man without heart or chest.[3] In his mature years, he was as shy and standoffish at a formal dance as he was playful and loving with the nieces and nephews whom he adored. But openness of manner was for him the exception and not the rule; Madison was respected by virtually all of his contemporaries and intimately known by only a few. As a keen student of human nature once observed, though, the most "acute and retentive" human feelings seldom belong to one who makes a parade of speeches and emotions. They are more at home in the soul of "quiet grandeur."[4]

The period 1776–1800 is one of the most remarkable and engrossing stories of a nation's founding. Unlike the legendary foundings of the republics of antiquity, there was no single lawgiver who, after completing his work, retired to a distant land. Instead, the period following the establishment of the new American Constitution was stamped by the dramatic interplay among the diverse characters of the Founding generation and the force of their ideas. Despite his unassuming nature, Madison played as large a part in the drama of the early American republic as any of the Founders and a larger role than most of them. He served in many elected positions in Virginia and

---

[2] "Spirit of Governments," *PJM* 14:234.

[3] See C. S. Lewis's chapter, "Men Without Chests," in *The Abolition of Man* (New York: HarperCollins, 2001).

[4] See Jane Austen, *Emma*, in *The Complete Novels of Jane Austen*, 2 vols. (New York: Modern Library, 1992), 2:101; Leo Strauss, *What Is Political Philosophy?* (Westport, Conn.: Greenwood Press, 1959), 103–4.

the United States, including in the United States House of Representatives, as Jefferson's secretary of state, and, of course, as the fourth president of the United States. He was the leading man of ideas at the Constitutional Convention of 1787 and coauthored with Alexander Hamilton (and a minimal contribution from John Jay) *The Federalist*, which Jefferson called "the best commentary on the principles of government which ever was written."[5]

Only a short time later, however, he and Hamilton would be on the political outs, with Madison acting as the leading voice of the republican opposition to the Hamiltonian-led Federalist political and economic program. As a result of the party battles of the 1790s and Hamilton's influence with President Washington, Madison would ultimately find himself estranged from the president for whom he had previously acted as penman of his most important official addresses and speeches, including the First Inaugural Address.[6] The rupture would be a matter of some sadness for Madison, for Washington was a man he deeply esteemed. Despite his fundamental disagreements with Hamilton, he never ceased to respect him as well, particularly for the power of his mind. The same could not be said of his opinion of John Adams – one of the few men whose ideas as well as character Madison criticized quite harshly, albeit privately. Madison's early affiliation with Jefferson in Virginia politics grew into a deep and abiding personal friendship and political alliance that lasted throughout their lives.

Except for a hiatus during the late 1790s and early 1800s, the very different personalities and political views of Jefferson and John Adams did not stand in the way of a long and ultimately enduring friendship between them. Indeed, their work together on the committee that drafted the Declaration of Independence in 1776 came full circle on July 4, 1826, when the revolutionary collaborators died within hours of each other. If Jefferson and Adams were political enemies but personal friends, Adams and Hamilton shared many of the same political views and most of the same political opponents, but they were never friends; on more than one occasion, they were intraparty enemies. Madison's regard for Hamilton's intellect was paralleled by Jefferson's appreciation of Adams's revolutionary principles; Madison's dislike of Adams found common but harsher ground in Jefferson's detestation of Hamilton, which Hamilton returned in kind. The description of the relationships among the dramatis personae in the 1790s' political playbook reads a bit like a variation on the theme of *A Midsummer Night's Dream*,

---

[5] Jefferson to Madison, November 18, 1788, *PJM* 11:353.
[6] For an excellent treatment of the friendship between Washington and Madison see Stuart Leibiger, *Founding Friendship* (Charlottesville: University of Virginia Press, 2001).

though Washington, try as he might, was not able to conjure up Puck's power of the honest neighbor who makes them all friends.

Still, Madison's role in the drama of the American Founding is one thing, but what about Madison the man? The itch to come to know the Founders is, for many of us, the desire to come to know them personally. As in the case of great artists, we are often not satisfied with knowing them through their chosen form of self-revelation; we want to know them directly, to see into their souls.[7] But this is not always possible. In the case of the philosopher and writer, for example, often we come to know them better in the stories they told than in the stories that can be told about them. This, I think, is the way it is with Madison. Madison made a significant contribution in all of the political posts he held, but it is in the capacity of political thinker that he made the deepest and most indelible impression on our nation. As much as and perhaps more than any of the Founders, he thought through the original vision of the new republic and transformed it into reality. In a sense, his story is the story of an idea – the idea of America.

Americans are a people with a distinctive way of life that sets them apart from other peoples. With the French, or Chinese, or Iraqis, or Somalis, we share a common humanity and many of the same miseries and hopes. But we do not all love or hate the same things. We do not have all of the same principles or prejudices. Like individuals, each nation has a particular character and a unique story. To tell the story of a nation well, there must be a narrator who is able to see through the events and the details on the surface to the spirit that moves it and gives it its character. In *The Mind of the Maker*, Dorothy L. Sayers brilliantly captures the forces at work behind the creation of a story. In the art of writing, as in Christianity, she argues, there is a trinitarian structure that underlies the work. This consists of the idea, the activity, and the power. Behind the finished work (and the activity that produced it) is a creative idea that has the potential power to set all else in motion. The power proceeds from the idea and the activity together and is the means by which the work is communicated to others. It is the link that connects the immaterial idea to its material manifestation and brings the work to life.[8] "The Power – the Spirit – is . . . a social power, working to bring all minds into its own unity. . . ."[9] This same structure,

---

[7] See Dorothy L. Sayers, *The Mind of the Maker* (San Francisco: Harcourt, Brace and Company, 1941), 57.

[8] In Christianity the idea, the activity, and the power are indicative of the Father, the Son, and the Holy Spirit or the Word, the Flesh, and the Holy Spirit. The Word is made Flesh (the incarnation) by the power of the Holy Spirit. See John 1:14; cf. the Apostle's Creed.

[9] Sayers, *Mind of the Maker*, 131.

Sayers argues, is present in all forms of artistic creation and in fact in the mind of man. There is, for example, a trinitarian structure in human sight, consisting of the form seen, the act of seeing it, and the mental attention or power that correlates the two. These things are as separable in theory as they are inseparably present in the experience of sight.

I would argue that this same threefold pattern is at work in political life, particularly in the creative act of founding a new nation. What Sayers designates "idea," "activity," and "power" (or "spirit"), Aristotle called "principle," "ethos," and "spirit." To understand a given political order, Aristotle taught, we must look beyond the political surface of the laws and see that there is a distinctive ethos that characterizes it. This activity, or way of life, is informed by a particular principle or idea. Between the principle and the activity there is a bridge that links them together, which we might call the "spirit" of the community. In free societies, this spirit finds expression in public opinion. This notion has been explored in our time by scholars such as Edward S. Corwin and A. D. Lindsay, who have argued for the importance of attending to the operative opinion that informs the political order and gives it life and force. According to Corwin, the regime, or constitution in the formal sense, is the "nucleus of a set of ideas."[10] To understand a nation, Lindsay argued, one must primarily concern oneself "with the ideals which are actually operative – operative enough in men's minds to make them go on obeying a particular form of government or, at times, to make them break up the government they are accustomed to and try to construct a new one."[11]

This dynamic conception of politics marked the mind of Madison. To know him, we must come to understand his vision of America and the story he wrote in his mind before it was written upon the land. Madison's narrative was informed by the idea of republican self-government, whose manifestation he sought to bring about in the way of life of the American people. He believed that this could not be accomplished without the link that connects the idea of self-government to the ethos of republicanism. He called

[10] Edward S. Corwin, *American Constitutional History* (New York: Harper and Row, 1954), 101.

[11] A. D. Lindsay, *The Modern Democratic State* (New York: Oxford University Press, 1962), 37. It is interesting to note that Lindsay edited a reissue of William Ellis's renowned translation of Aristotle's *A Treatise on Government*, an earlier edition of which was owned and studied by James Madison. In his introduction to this work, Lindsay argued that in the view of Plato and Aristotle, "no private education can hold out against the irresistible force of public opinion and the ordinary moral standards of society. But that makes it all the more essential that public opinion and social environment should not be left to grow up at haphazard as they ordinarily do.... "

this link the "spirit" of republican government. When released, this spirit is communicated to others through public opinion and results in certain intellectual and moral habits; it is the means by which the idea becomes an active energy that generates a process of republican self-renewal.

Such an approach to understanding the human arts, whether that of writing or music or sculpture or politics, is grounded in a view of human nature and human life that is dynamic and in which the phenomenon cannot be properly treated by a purely scientific, mechanical approach that merely devises a "solution" to a "problem." "We can see St. Paul's Cathedral purely in terms of the problems solved by the architect," Sayers contends,

[in] the calculations of stress and strain imposed by the requirements of the site. But there is nothing there that will tell us why men were willing to risk death to save St. Paul's from destruction; or why the bomb that crashed through its roof was felt by millions like a blow over the heart.[12]

One need only recall the well-known photograph of St. Paul's Cathedral during the December 1940 bombing of London to know what Sayers means. Or perhaps the image of the twin towers of New York, now no longer standing but indelibly burnt upon the American mind, furnishes our generation the picture Sayers painted in words for an earlier one. Not every challenge that we are faced with in life is a problem to be solved. Sometimes what is before us is the challenge of a work to be made.[13] If we fail to recognize the potential power of an idea or a principle to inspire the souls and actions of human beings, we will not be able to understand the mind of Madison, any more than we would be able to understand a Washington or a Lincoln or a Churchill, or the citizens who gave their lives in the wars over which they presided.

This power is rooted in the freedom of the human mind and will. The nature of human freedom is precisely what allows for, indeed calls for, a creative idea that has the power to inspire and guide it. This is the task of the creator, but it is one that has certain natural laws and limits. A parent creates a child, a writer creates a character. A Founder creates a nation – a people. But like the parent or literary artist, the Founder can have only partial control over what he has created. He must recognize the essential freedom of mind and will of the characters he has formed. His own freedom consists in applying his energy to the form and limits of the medium within which he works so that it is not wrenched from the process of development

---

[12] Sayers, *Mind of the Maker*, 193–94.
[13] Ibid., 181–216.

that is natural to it. "The business of the creator is not to escape from his material medium or to bully it," Sayers argues, "but to serve it," and "to serve it he must love it."[14]

In the first of his *Federalist* essays devoted to the character of the new government, Madison described the medium in which the Framers worked and the cause they served, as he understood it. "The genius of the people of America" and "the fundamental principles of the Revolution," he said, demand republican government. Only a genuine republic is reconcilable "with that honorable determination which animates every votary of freedom, to rest all our political experiments on the capacity of mankind for self-government."[15] For James Madison, to serve the cause of America meant to respect the freedom that cannot be taken from human beings without doing violence to their natures. To love the land and its people meant to cherish what they stood for and to trust in what they would become. This is the drama of self-government that Madison envisioned unfolding and wrapping around the minds and spirit of the American people. It is the story of the power of an idea.

[14] Ibid., 66.
[15] *Federalist* 39:208.

Introduction

Madison's Legacy

> The land was ours before we were the land's,
> She was our land more than a hundred years
> Before we were her people. She was ours
> In Massachusetts, in Virginia,
> But we were England's, still colonials,
> Possessing what we still were unpossessed by,
> Possessed by what we now no more possessed.
> Something we were withholding made us weak
> Until we found out that it was ourselves
> We were withholding from our land of living,
> And forthwith found salvation in surrender.
> Such as we were we gave ourselves outright
> (The deed of gift was many deeds of war)
> To the land vaguely realizing westward,
> But still unstoried, artless, unenhanced,
> Such as she was, such as she would become.
> > Robert Frost, "The Gift Outright"

At President John F. Kennedy's inauguration in 1961, the capital blanketed with freshly fallen snow and capped by a glaring winter's sun, Robert Frost was scheduled to read his newly composed poem "Dedication." The conditions made it impossible for him to see the pages, so instead he delivered from memory an older verse about the birth of America – a poem, he once said, "about what Madison may have thought."[1] "The land was ours before

---

[1] Robert Frost, "An Extemporaneous Talk for Students," Sarah Lawrence College, June 7, 1956, in K. L. Knickbocker and H. Willard Reninger, eds., *Preliminaries to Literary Judgment: Interpreting Literature*, 5th ed. (New York: Holt Rinehart & Winston, 1974), 808. During this talk Frost remarked: "Now I thought I would say a poem to you – a poem about what Madison may have thought. This is called 'The Gift Outright' and it is my story of the

we were the land's." Later, in discovering within ourselves what had been withheld, we became the possession of the land. Frost's lines remind us of the ultimate sacrifice made by men whose bodies rest in soldiers' graves across the original thirteen states. They also evoke the cause to which our Founding generation gave themselves wholly. The Founders' legacy, like the soldiers' sacrifice, was a gift to future generations of Americans that could never be, and never was intended to be, repaid. It was "the gift outright."

A gift outright is a "deed of gift," which is "a deed executed and delivered without consideration," that is, with no expectation of return.[2] It is different from a legal contract, which sets terms of strict proportionality between benefits conferred and repayment required. Nonetheless, a deed of gift "confirms a legal relationship between the donor and repository that is based on trust and common understanding."[3] Thus, while no material repayment of the gift is required or expected, the legacy does confer on the recipients a moral obligation to respect the intended purpose of the bequest. Moreover, according to Aristotle, there are some gifts for which it is not possible to make equal payment, and that can be only partially, and rightfully, repaid by a debt of gratitude.[4] Aquinas calls the debt of gratitude a "debt of moral decency" that flows "from charity," which "the more it is paid, the more it is due."[5]

Frost's reminder of the gift we have received from our forefathers is also quietly, implicitly, a reminder to us of our debt. Calling to mind a time when the nation was "unstoried," when the original vision of the American drama was but an idea in Madison's imagination, he speaks to us today, the living beneficiaries of this still unfolding story. All through this poem about an event long past, there is no "they" but only and always "we." In surrendering to the land, we became "her people." Mingling the soil and the soul of America, Frost captures Madison's vision of a land populated by a sovereign and self-governing people. The gift of the American soldiers and Founders made us true proprietors, owned by a land that calls us to own

revolutionary war. My story of the revolutionary war might be about two little battles – one little battle called King's Mountain and another little battle called Bennington – but I'll leave battles out and give you the abstract."

[2] Bryan A. Garner, ed., *Black's Law Dictionary* (St. Paul, Minn: West Group, 1999), 423.

[3] http://www.archivists.org/publications/deed_of_gift.asp.

[4] Aristotle, *Nicomachean Ethics*, Martin Ostwald, trans. (New York: Macmillan Publishing Co., 1962), VIII:14, 244.

[5] Aquinas, *Summa Theologica* II-II Q. CVI ART. VI in *Aquinas Ethicas: Or, the Moral Teaching of St. Thomas*, 2 vols., Joseph Rickaby Thomas, ed. and trans. (New York: Benziger Bros., 1896), 2:201–2.

ourselves.[6] This idea was perfectly expressed by Tocqueville a generation later when he said, "I saw in America more than America."[7]

As much as, perhaps even more than, for their deeds of war and their deed of gift of independence, we are indebted to the Founding generation for the legacy of self-government they left to us. Madison understood his life's work as dedication to the crafting and constructing of this singular legacy. His contribution to the founding of the American republic was a deed of gift for which no equal payment is possible and for which recognition of his generosity is the fitting return of grateful souls. This gratitude, however, is contingent on understanding the worth of the benefit conveyed.[8] The debt we owe to the giver of qualitative goods requires more than giving honor to the benefactor; we must recognize and cherish the intrinsic good of the gift itself. For Madison, as well as for Frost, the legacy of the American Founders is best repaid not by statues and monuments to them, but by honoring the principles of republicanism they bequeathed to us. It is best repaid by the citizens' moral recognition of what we owe each other.

It has been said about Frost that he was "a philosopher, but [that] his ideas are behind his poems, not in them."[9] The power of "The Gift Outright" is only partially in the words that give meaning to the events of our past. Behind the words is a power that shapes our spirit and makes us into something more than mere readers. Only two years after Frost spoke at the 1961 inaugural, President Kennedy was called upon to commemorate the poet's death. "Our national strength matters," Kennedy said, "but the spirit which informs and controls our strength matters just as much. This was the special significance

---

[6] I am not unaware that my interpretation of Frost's ideas is at odds with a significant portion of the literary scholarship on the poet. While I do not wish to elide over the criticisms of Frost's own character or the darkness that may have haunted him, I do think the case can and should be made for Frost's command of his craft and for the deftness with which he captures and teaches the meaning of American democracy and the spirit that permeates it. Critics contend that this is a naive view set forth by those who do not understand poetry or Robert Frost, for Frost was a coward, a tyrant, and a liar through and through. I would suggest in response that poetry is not always about the poet, nor usually, if ever, written for the edification of literary critics. For a contrasting perspective see Lawrance Thompson, *Robert Frost*, 3 vols. (New York: Holt, Rinehart & Winston, 1966–76), and Robert Faggen, *Robert Frost and the Challenge of Darwinism* (Ann Arbor: University of Michigan Press, 2001). See also Jay Parini, *Robert Frost: A Life* (New York: Henry Holt and Co., 1999), who neither ignores Frost's shortcomings nor uses them to condemn his art or his civic aspirations (429).

[7] Alexis de Tocqueville, *Democracy in America*, J. P. Mayer, ed. (New York: Harper Perennial, 1969), 19.

[8] See Peter Chojnowski, "A Sense of Honor: Justice and Our Moral Debt," *Angelus* XXII (1999).

[9] Mark Van Doren, "The American Poet," *Atlantic Monthly* 187 (June 1951), 32–34.

of Robert Frost."¹⁰ This was also, I think, the special significance of James Madison. At the core of Frost's understanding of America was his insight into Madison's dream of a land informed and sustained by the spirit of a free people capable of controlling their government and governing themselves.

Frost's Madison is not the Madison we come to know in most of the scholarly literature. For the most part, the scholars' Madison is no friend of the common man. In the first part of the twentieth century Charles Beard's Progressive interpretation of Madison dominated the scholarly landscape, portraying Madison as an opponent of democracy and a destroyer of the principles of the American Revolution.¹¹ In the mid-twentieth century, under the scholarly leadership of Martin Diamond, Madison became the Founder who sought to institute a system of clever mechanistic political arrangements that make it possible to dispense with civic education and the need to form an American character.¹² This Madison is a democratic liberal who established a system of pluralistic, interest-dominated politics. By thwarting the formation and influence of majorities in the extended republic, he created a governmental machine that turned private vice into public good. J. G. A. Pocock and Gordon Wood attacked this thesis with weapons stockpiled in the historians' arsenal, situating Madison within the classical republican tradition that began in ancient Greece and continued through Machiavelli and into the era of the American Founding.¹³ Aristocratic leadership and deferential politics are the mainstay in this view of Madisonian politics, achieved

---

¹⁰ President John F. Kennedy, Remarks at Amherst College, October 26, 1963, in Robert G. Torricelli and Andrew Carroll, eds., *In Our Own Words: Extraordinary Speeches of the American Century* (New York: Kodansha International, 1999), 242.

¹¹ Charles A. Beard, *An Economic Interpretation of the Constitution of the United States* (New York: Free Press, [1913] 1986). For a powerful critique of Beard's thesis, see Forrest McDonald, *We the People: The Economic Origins of the Constitution* (Chicago: University of Chicago Press, 1958), and Robert E. Brown, *Charles Beard and the Constitution: A Critical Analysis of "An Economic Interpretation of the Constitution"* (Princeton, N.J.: Princeton University Press, 1956). See also contemporary Progressive interpretations of Madisonian theory in the work of Richard K. Matthews, *If Men Were Angels: James Madison & the Heartless Empire of Reason* (Lawrence: University Press of Kansas, 1995); Jennifer Nedelski, *Private Property and the Limits of American Constitutionalism: The Madisonian Framework and Its Legacy* (Chicago: University of Chicago Press, 1990); Woody Holton, "'Divide et Impera': *Federalist* 10 in a Wider Sphere," *William and Mary Quarterly* 62 (2005), 175–212.

¹² See William A. Schambra, ed., *As Far as Republican Principles Will Admit: Essays by Martin Diamond* (Washington, D.C.: AEI Press, 1992). The interpretation of Madison as a pluralist theorist continues into the present; see, for example, Steven D. Smith, *The Constitution and the Pride of Reason* (New York: Oxford University Press, 1998), 67–68.

¹³ Gordon Wood, "Interests and Disinterestedness in the Making of the Constitution," in Richard Beeman, Stephen Botein, and Edward C. Carter, eds., *Beyond Confederation: Origins of the Constitution and American National Identity* (Chapel Hill: University of North Carolina Press, 1987), 91–93; Gordon Wood, *The Creation of the American Republic,*

in part by an extended territory composed of large congressional districts conducive to electing the better sorts of men. At present, the synthesis theory, or "multiple traditions approach" theory, to Madison is prevalent, which attempts to blend the liberal democratic and classical republican schools of thought. Michael Zuckert and Alan Gibson, for example, contend that there are classical elements in Madison's thought, but that the modern liberal ideas of natural rights, limited government, and economic freedom are the predominant strains of his political theory.[14]

In each of these interpretive camps there are scholars who rigorously call into question Madison's democratic credentials. This includes the modern liberal and many of the synthesis interpretations in one significant respect. Like the antidemocratic liberalism of contemporary Progressive scholars (e.g., Jennifer Nedelsky and Woody Holton) or the antidemocratic republicanism of Gordon Wood and others, they claim that Madison's remedy for the problem of majority faction in the 10th *Federalist* was intended to make it virtually impossible for the people to form a collective judgment. An extensive territory composed of a multiplicity of interests and parties not only deters the formation of a majority faction, but in general makes it difficult for the people to communicate effectively and to discover a common opinion. The doctrine of separation of powers increases the difficulty of forming a majority consensus on any given issue. The antidemocratic thesis takes this further: Madison's paean to popular sovereignty was in reality a death knell for popular government, these scholars claim. While some of these scholars contend that Madison's aim was to deadlock democracy,[15] others argue that his object was an end run around democracy. According to Wood, for example, though Madison and his Federalist cohorts couched their arguments in

---

1776–1787 (Chapel Hill: University of North Carolina Press, 1969), 510–18. See also Garry Wills, *Explaining America: The Federalist* (Garden City, N.Y.: Doubleday, 1981), 179–294; James Roger Sharp, *American Politics in the Early Republic: The New Nation in Crisis* (New Haven, Conn.: Yale University Press, 1993), 26.

[14] See Michael P. Zuckert, *The Natural Rights Republic: Studies in the Foundation of the American Political Tradition* (Notre Dame, Ind.: University of Notre Dame Press, 1996), especially ch. 7; Alan Gibson, *Interpreting the American Founding: Guide to the Enduring Debates over the Origins and Foundations of the American Republic* (Lawrence: University of Kansas Press, 2006), passim, especially ch. 6; Alan Gibson, *Understanding the Founding: The Crucial Questions* (Lawrence: University Press of Kansas, 2007), chs. 4 and 5. These two recent works by Gibson constitute the best literature review of scholarship on the American Founding period. Gibson follows the diverse scholarly interpretations of the Founding through a labyrinth of ideas, allowing the reader to emerge with an understanding that is at once cogent and complex, varied and ongoing. In this volume, I have deliberately not attempted to repeat the work Gibson has so recently and expertly done.

[15] See Robert A. Dahl, *A Preface to Democratic Theory* (Chicago: University of Chicago Press, 1956).

democratic language, they actually (and disingenuously) used democratic rhetoric to establish and justify an aristocratic system. Separating the social authority of the people and the political authority of the government, the Federalists imagined the Constitution as a "sort of 'philosopher's stone'" that could "transmute base materials into gold...."[16] According to Joshua Miller, Madison conceived of the sovereignty of the people in abstract terms and undermined the democratic principles of the American Revolution. By dispensing with the need for civic participation and thwarting communicative activity among the citizenry, Madison created a "ghostly body politic."[17]

In addition to the classical republican versus modern liberal theses and the democratic versus antidemocratic strains of interpretation, the issue of Madison's consistency of thought is a matter of great scholarly contention. The vast majority of historians and political theorists addressing the issue have concluded that in the 1790s Madison switched sides from his nationalist stance in the 1780s to a more Jeffersonian states' rights position, demonstrating a mind mired in confusion and inconsistency, or perhaps even one suffering from schizophrenia or tainted by dishonesty. Most of these interpretations have focused on Madison's contributions to *The Federalist* to expound his essential views, with perhaps a skimming of his writings in the 1790s to show that he changed his mind.

In recent years, a handful of scholars have attempted to move beyond an overconcentration on the 10th *Federalist* as the telling account of Madison's political theory and to present a more accurate and nuanced picture of his ideas.[18] The careful work of Lance Banning stands out particularly in this regard. In *The Sacred Fire of Liberty: James Madison & the Founding of the Federal Republic,*[19] Banning traces the development of Madison's founding vision throughout the 1780s and 1790s and has successfully shown, I think,

---

[16] Wood, *The Creation of the American Republic, 1776–1787,* 562, 475, 507.

[17] Joshua Miller, "The Ghostly Body Politic: The Federalist Papers and Popular Sovereignty," *Political Theory* 16 (1988), 99–119.

[18] For a more detailed treatment of the recent scholarly literature on the issue of Madison's consistency or inconsistency of thought, see Alan Gibson, "The Madisonian Madison and the Question of Consistency: The Consistency and Challenge of Recent Research," *The Review of Politics* 64:2 (2002), 311–38. Gibson identifies Irving Brant, Martin Diamond, Gordon Wood, and John Zvesper as the leading claimants of the view that Madison was inconsistent and Drew McCoy, Gary Rosen, James Read, Michael Zuckert, Jack Rakove, and Lance Banning as the foremost voices defending Madison's consistency. In *Revolutionary Characters: What Made the Founders Different* (New York: Penguin Press, 2006, 141–72), however, Gordon Wood vigorously makes the case for Madison's consistency and that there is no "'Madison problem,' except the one we [historians] have concocted."

[19] Lance Banning, *The Sacred Fire of Liberty: James Madison & the Founding of the Federal Republic* (Ithaca, N.Y.: Cornell University Press, 1995); cf. Banning, *Conceived in Liberty: The Struggle to Define the New Republic, 1789–1993* (Lanham, Md.: Rowman & Littlefield, 2004).

that scholars have generally misunderstood Madison's conception of federal republicanism and thus have erroneously concluded that he changed from a Hamiltonian-type nationalist distrustful of the power of the states and of the people in the 1780s to a states' righter and Jeffersonian democrat in the 1790s. According to Banning, throughout the Founding period, indeed throughout his life, Madison was consistently concerned about both the problem of majority faction and the threat of governmental tyranny. In the 1790s he did not change his principles; rather, he changed his emphasis. In the 1780s he concentrated on the problem of majority faction; in the 1790s, as a result of Hamilton's and the Federalists' attempt to increase the power of the national government at the expense of the authority of the states and the people, he concentrated on the problem of a powerful minority faction within the government. "Madison's lifelong concern," Marvin Meyers asserts, "has sometimes obscured the source of that concern: his prior commitment to popular government."[20] In sum, Madison consciously and consistently devoted himself to securing the democratic principles of the Revolution, the liberty of individuals, and the standard of self-government in the new federal republic.

While there is a substantial scholarly literature on Madison's political theory in the Constitutional Convention and *The Federalist*, relatively few studies have been devoted to his political theory and practice at the outset of the new government, and there is no book-length examination of his major theoretical writings during this period, viz., the "Notes on Government" and his essays for the *National Gazette*, or Party Press Essays.[21] Yet the

---

[20] Marvin Meyers, *The Mind of the Founder: Sources of Political Thought of James Madison* (Hanover, N.H.: Brandeis University Press, 1981), 408.

[21] See, for example, William B. Allen, "Justice and the General Good: *Federalist* 51," in Charles R. Kesler, ed., *Saving the Revolution: The Federalist Papers and the American Founding* (New York: Free Press, 1987), 133–36; John Zvesper, "The Madisonian Systems," *The Western Political Quarterly* 37:2 (1984), 236–56; Douglas W. Jaenicke, "Madison v. Madison: The Party Press Essays v. The Federalist Papers," in Richard Maidment and John Zvesper, eds., *Reflections on the Constitution: The American Constitution After Two Hundred Years* (New York: Manchester University Press, 1989), 116–47; Matthews, *If Men Were Angels*, 158–64; Banning, *Sacred Fire of Liberty*, 348–61; Gary Rosen, *American Compact: James Madison and the Problem of Founding* (Lawrence: University Press of Kansas, 1999), 152–55; Saul Cornell, *The Other Founders: Anti-Federalism & the Dissenting Tradition in America, 1788–1828* (Chapel Hill: University of North Carolina Press, 1999), 166–68, 247–53; James H. Read, *Power versus Liberty: Madison, Hamilton, Wilson, and Jefferson* (Charlottesville: University Press of Virginia, 2000), 32, 45; Larry D. Kramer, *The People Themselves: Popular Constitutionalism and Judicial Review* (Oxford: Oxford University Press, 2004), 112–14; Larry D. Kramer, "The Interest of the Man: James Madison, Popular Constitutionalism, and the Theory of Deliberative Democracy," *Valparaiso University Law Review*, 41:2 (2007), 697–754; Alan Gibson, "Veneration and Vigilance: James Madison and Public Opinion," *Review of Politics* 67:1 (2005), 5–35, 69–76; Todd Estes, "Shaping

years 1791–92 were perhaps the most intense period of philosophic activity in Madison's life. This study focuses on Madison's political thought and actions during the decade of the 1790s, with particular emphasis on his writings of 1791–92.

By the spring of 1791, after the close of the first Congress in which he served, Madison's concerns over the future of the new nation had intensified as a result of John Adams's influential publications and the passage of Alexander Hamilton's bill to establish a national bank in the United States. During this spring Madison spent a concentrated period of time engrossed in the study of political philosophy and history, taking extensive notes on numerous sources and composing a detailed outline that treats the central political concerns in a remarkably comprehensive manner. Later that year and into the next, he published a series of nineteen articles in the *National Gazette* (many of which were reprinted in other newspapers) that reflected some of these concerns and are every bit as theoretically interesting and provocative as the essays he penned under the pseudonym Publius. These Party Press Essays defined the "republican cause" of the 1790s in America and established Madison as the principal philosophic proponent of the newly emerging Republican Party. To the role of philosophic leader Madison conjoined that of political leader of the Republicans, who set themselves in opposition to the policy agenda emanating from the office of the secretary of the treasury. In defining the republican cause and leading the opposition to Hamilton's political, economic, and foreign policy program, Madison did more than anyone else – except perhaps Hamilton – to cause the first great political fissure in the American republic. The feud between Republicans and Federalists in the 1790s left a lasting impression on the American political landscape. It marked the formation of the first political parties in the United States, led to the decisive victory of the Republicans over the Federalists in the election of 1800, and established, at least for a time, a tradition of participatory politics in the American republic.

Although it is one of the most noted political battles of American history, the cause of this dispute remains to this day a source of confusion and controversy among scholars. The majority of scholars have concluded that in the 1790s Madison simply changed his mind about the theory of republican

the Politics of Public Opinion: Federalists and the Jay Treaty," *Journal of the Early Republic* 20:3 (2000), 393–423; Estes, *The Jay Treaty Debate, Public Opinion, and the Evolution of Early American Culture* (Amherst: University of Massachusetts Press, 2006), 7–8, and passim.

government that he presented in the pages of *The Federalist*, Banning being the foremost exception to this view. When Madison was confronted with the charge of inconsistency during his own lifetime, he denied that he had undergone any material change of mind.[22] I would suggest that Banning's arguments should be more heeded, and that a solid understanding of the motives and views behind Madison's alleged switch of positions between the late 1780s and the early 1790s requires more than a juxtaposition of the much-studied ideas of Publius with a cursory view of Madison's arguments in the first administration. Indeed, I believe that a careful examination of his writings of the 1790s provides a revealing account of Madison's philosophic self-understanding and the reasons he deliberately waged war against the Federalist agenda.

Madison's criticisms of John Adams's brand of republicanism and Hamilton's political and economic policies were not ad hoc, nor was Madison's intent simply to oppose Federalist measures. The battles he waged against Federalist policies were grounded in a positive republican vision and a constructive agenda as well. In Madison's mind, the arguments he laid out and the policies he pursued at the outset of the new government were tied together by a central philosophical idea – the fundamental authority of the people and the sovereignty of public opinion in free government. In his conception of republicanism, adherence to the form and spirit of popular government in the new nation meant the recognition of the supremacy of the Constitution, understood and administered in a manner consistent with the sense of the people who ratified and adopted it. It also meant the *ongoing* sovereignty of public opinion, which requires the active participation of the citizenry in the affairs of the political community.

In Madison's perception, the Federalists of the 1790s were attempting to craft a highly energetic and independent status for the executive, create a narrow governmental dependence on the wealthy few, and limit the citizenry to a submissive role based merely on their "confidence in government." Rejecting this schema, Madison advocated the politics of public opinion, through which he sought to foster and form an enlightened and broadly based public voice that would control and direct the measures of government.[23] While he

---

[22] See Madison to N. P. Trist, September 27, 1834, *WJM* 9:471–77.

[23] William B. Allen argues that contrary to the Federalist view that the Constitution was grounded in a "political system founded on public opinion and the institutions of which, once established, constituted the very expression of public opinion," Madison and Jefferson believed that the Constitution had "erected a political system founded on but therefore subject to popular opinion. Accordingly, the offices and officers of the United States owed special deference and respect to popular opinion, and it would be appropriate to provide a

did not deny to political leaders and enlightened men a critical place in the formation of public opinion, he fought vehemently against the Federalists' thin version of the politics of public opinion. In opposition to the Hamiltonian view of an economically absorbed and politically subservient people, he advanced the image of a responsible citizenry (composed primarily of sturdy, independent yeoman farmers) with an active and substantial role in republican government. He believed as well that ascertaining the real opinion of the public would unmask those Federalists who sought to counterfeit public opinion and use their version of it to separate Washington from the vast republican majority in America.

Although Madison's particular conception of participatory politics was intended to avert the problem of the tyranny of the majority, it nonetheless encouraged the communication of the citizens' views and the formation of a united public voice, thereby widening the path of opportunity for the power of public opinion. In the view of many Federalists, this threatened the checks on majoritarian politics contrived by the Framers; it asked more of the people than they could responsibly contribute to political life. Madison too was well aware of the potential dangers associated with majority opinion; in fact, none of the Founders was more mindful of such dangers. Nevertheless, he consciously took upon himself the role of chief philosophic architect and political leader of the republican effort to institute the politics of public opinion in America.

The communication of ideas and the refinement of views throughout the land, he claimed, can result in the attainment of "the reason of the public" and is the republican way to achieve impartiality in government. Federalists reacted with contempt and ultimately alarm to this brand of politics and the worship of the "Goddess of Reason." It sounded to them like the naive democratic optimism and "vain reveries of a false and new fangled philosophy" coming out of the French Enlightenment. Madison did not dispute the claim of French Enlightenment influence. Since the latter part of the 1780s Jefferson had been sending Madison crates of books by French authors on public opinion, and Madison had indeed been avidly reading their thoughts on the subject.

special conveyance outside of government for the expression of that opinion. The struggle over the question, whether the opinion of the people prevailed *in* or *over* the government gave rise to that party debate which to this date provides the pure form of all political disputes in the United States" ("The Constitution to End All Constitutions: The Descent of the American Founding into the Twentieth Century, or The Perfect State Is Not Ideal," 8–9, http://www.msu.edu/~allenwi/presentations/Constitution_to_End_all_Constitutions).

From his opening salvo in the *National Gazette* in the fall of 1791, Madison viewed the battles of the 1790s as rooted in a philosophic difference of opinion about the principles and conditions of republican government. In time, many of his opponents also came to believe that these political battles stemmed from more than merely partisan bickering. Ultimately, they acknowledged that they were engaged in a war of ideas that would essentially determine the character and fate of republicanism in America.

The war of ideas that marked the political landscape of America in the 1790s was part of, indeed grew out of, a larger disagreement within European Enlightenment thought in the eighteenth century. In the European conflict, the advocates of the politics of public opinion lined up on one side and launched an offensive attack against the more established proponents of the theory of mixed and balanced government. The older school of thought was concentrated in Great Britain, while the later strand of Enlightenment thought developed primarily, but not solely, in France. In reaction to both of these conceptions of politics, a third strand of thought emerged in the ancien régime, loosely embodied by men who opposed the new rationalism and who sought to reclaim what they considered the richer and more dynamic approach to politics that characterized the classical political philosophers. Following Jonathan Swift's lively depiction of the Archimedean struggle in *The Battle of the Books*, they traced the source of their philosophic rivals' ideas back to Descartes and Hobbes and the conscious break with classical political philosophy (or even further back to Machiavelli's rejection of classical as well as Christian thought). In the eighteenth century, new terms were added to the contest, including those found in the pages of Locke, Hume, and Rousseau. To a significant extent, however, the battle of ideas was reincited and reframed by the majestic and controversial work of the Baron de Montesquieu, Charles-Louis de Secondat, *The Spirit of Laws*. Montesquieu's penetrating analysis of forms of governments and the various factors that determine the character of political societies attracted a host of followers and critics. His work became, as it were, the battleground for eighteenth-century political thought, though given the complexity and subtlety of his analysis, there was no simple alignment of troops. Many writers and politicians took what appealed to them in his work and rejected or ignored the remainder, often attempting to take Montesquieu's ideas further than he perhaps would have been willing to go.

Madison developed his theory of republicanism within the context of these opposing schools of Enlightenment thought, set against the broader background of the battle between the ancients and the moderns. Given his consciousness of the larger debate and his references to it in his writings of the 1790s, attention to the intellectual context within which Madison thought and wrote is critically important to understanding his ideas during this era. Moreover, an examination of the patterns of thought with which he was thoroughly familiar and to which he reacted, rather than the creation of new and foreign ones, may well contribute to a better understanding and more vivid picture of Madison's political theory than has heretofore been made available.

More than any of the other Founding Fathers, Madison is credited with thinking through and designing the constitutional blueprint for the United States. Yet there are fewer studies of his life and ideas than of those of the other leading Founders. This volume is devoted to exploring the way of life James Madison envisioned for America. Because the primary aim of the work is to grasp Madison's vision of republicanism, followed by the effort to understand how his ideas informed his actions, the themes of the book are arranged dialectically rather than chronologically. This approach allows the reader to see more clearly the logic and interconnectedness of Madison's various arguments and actions throughout the early Founding era; at the same time, it is hoped, it does not sacrifice the historical and political to the intellectual context. Chapter 1 provides an overview of Madison's opposition politics in 1791–92, beginning with his research on the "Notes on Government" in the spring of 1791 and following the contours of his argument through the Party Press Essays. In the earlier Essays, Madison criticized the Federalist agenda and defined the "republican cause"; by the spring of 1792 he was openly championing the emergence of the Republican Party. Chapter 2 begins by stepping back in history, setting forth the context in which Madison developed his ideas and pursued his political goals in the early 1790s. The views and policies of two of the Federalist leaders, viz., Vice President John Adams and Secretary of the Treasury Alexander Hamilton, at whom Madison's criticisms were largely (albeit often implicitly) directed, are examined here, particularly their laudatory view of the British model of government. Chapter 3 further broadens the context in which Madison thought and wrote, examining late-eighteenth-century French authors whom he studied and whose ideas clearly influenced his thinking during this period, including their censure of the British constitution and their development of the theory of the politics of public opinion.

Chapter 4 examines the affirmative theory of republicanism Madison presented in the "Notes on Government" and Party Press Essays, demonstrating how the various components of his republican theory fit together to form a cohesive whole. This presentation includes the well-known foundational elements of Madisonian theory, that is, the extended republic, representation, separation of powers, checks and balances, and federalism. It also incorporates his arguments and analysis in the 1790s' materials, thereby contributing to a fuller and richer account of Madisonian republican theory. In particular, his conception of the theory of public opinion and his advocacy of the commerce of ideas throughout the extended republic are highlighted and analyzed, showing the nonmechanistic and human face of Madison's political vision. In these writings, the stress on the importance of civic education and the need to form republican habits of mind and heart reveal the conception of politics at the core of his republican ideas. Chapter 5 applies Madison's theory of public opinion to his stance on the dominant political issues of the Washington administration, viz., a bill of rights, the funding of the national debt, the proposal to establish a national bank, Hamilton's Report on Manufactures, commercial discrimination, and the president's Neutrality Proclamation.

Chapter 6 continues the application of Madisonian theory to practice during the Adams administration, most notably his stance on the Alien and Sedition Acts. Jefferson's views in this controversy are also examined here. In addition, the philosophic similarities and differences between Madison and Jefferson during the 1790s are explored, with attention to Jefferson's Draft Constitution for Virginia, his theory of generational sovereignty, Madison's 49th and 50th *Federalist* essays, and his response to Jefferson's letter regarding the "Earth Belongs to the Living Generation." In regard to practical politics in the 1790s, more often than not, the founding and leadership of the Republican Party are generally attributed to Jefferson, with Madison treated as the Sundance Kid to Jefferson's Butch Cassidy. In Chapter 6, I argue that this is not an accurate account of the practical or philosophic origins of the Republican Party or of their relationship to each other. In the early 1790s, Madison acted as the philosophic leader of the Republican cause and the practical leader of the Republican Party; Jefferson took over in 1797 when he became vice president and Madison (temporarily) retired to Montpelier.

Chapter 7 provides a summary view of Madison's 1791 "Notes on Government," developing more fully the character of political analysis and the nature of the political task in which Madison understood himself to be engaged. Because of the broad and comprehensive nature of Madison's inquiry in this notebook and his continued investigation into the general theme of the "Notes" later in his life, I have placed this subject near the end of the volume. This material abounds with citations of ancient and modern historians and political philosophers and is particularly helpful in conceptualizing the context in which Madison developed his own theory of republican government. Aristotle's notion of public opinion and the spirit of governments, Montesquieu's reformulation of Aristotle's thesis, and Madison's analysis of this subject provide the focus for this chapter. In situating his analysis of the influences on government, and republican government in particular, within the context of "the great oracles of political wisdom," Madison's "Notes" offer a window into his thinking about politics that takes us beyond the accumulated studies of Madisonian theory. At the very least, the "Notes on Government" deserve the attention devoted to them in this study, and probably a great deal more.[24] I conclude this chapter with a discussion of how we might rethink the categories of analysis that have been generally applied to Madisonian political thought, suggesting that Madison himself would not accept the overly abstract and insufficiently political approach that is so often employed by scholars today. Rather, he consciously rejected the scientific rationalism and the merely institutional mechanical approach of his time and sought instead to reclaim the richer and more political approach to regime analysis that marked a long tradition of "oracles of political wisdom."

Finally, in the Epilogue, the question of the relevance of Madison's ideas today is set forth for readers' consideration. In a land that now extends from sea to sea and includes over 300 million people, is the kind of participatory, self-governing citizenship along the lines that Madison envisioned possible? Is it desirable? Or was this merely a whimsical dream by the Father of our Constitution whose time has come and gone? In the twentieth century, the man who posed this question most forcefully and eloquently was Robert Frost. In his response Frost provides less of an answer for us than a challenge to us, but it is a challenge that may be worth more than the scholar's answer or even the philosopher's stone.

---

[24] Although I originally intended to include a more extensive treatment of the "Notes on Government" in this volume, the breadth of Madison 's research project and the somewhat lengthy exegesis that the material requires led me to conclude that it would be better to provide an in-depth treatment of the "Notes on Government" in a separate volume. I intend to present this treatment in *Madison's Voyage to the World of the Classics.*

I

Republican Opposition

It was one of those pleasant Philadelphia days in early spring when the wind changes direction to a southwesterly and folks of every age and description, shut indoors over the cold and frosty winter months, venture forth to enjoy the awakening of nature.[1] At noon on March 13 a horse and carriage party of family and friends was seen driving forth for a "wade into the country."[2] Two gentlemen, one tall and lean, with burnished copper hair and an alluring personality to match, the other substantially smaller, younger, shier, and dressed in black (as was his wont), formed part of the cheerful assembly. Best friends for many years, they had first met and formed a lasting bond when they were in public service together in their native Virginia. Now, after a hiatus of five years during which the vast expanse of the Atlantic Ocean had separated them, they were delighted to be in each other's company once again.

The year was 1791. The day was Sunday. The gentlemen riding in the light breeze under a fair midday sun were Thomas Jefferson and James Madison. The former served as secretary of state in the Washington administration, having two months prior returned from service as minister to the court of Louis XVI in Paris, France. The other had only ten days ago completed his first term in the House of Representatives of the United States under the new Constitution. Following the pleasures of their country outing, the little band of sightseers reassembled at Mr. Jefferson's table in the late afternoon. After dinner, Madison ambled the short distance back to his residence at

---

[1] Charles Peirce, *A Meteorological Account of the Weather in Philadelphia: from January 1, 1790, to January 1, 1847* (Philadelphia: Lindsay & Blakiston, 1847), 51. I would like to thank Jacqueline Mirabile of Falvey Library, Villanova University, for her kind assistance in helping me locate these data.

[2] Jefferson to Madison, March 13, 1791, *PJM* 13:404.

15

Mrs. House's Boarding House on Fifth and Market, where, we suppose, he resumed his morning studies. Since the adjournment of Congress, he had set himself a "little task" that would consume his time and energy for a number of weeks, probably until late April, when he removed to New York to prepare for a respite northward. In May, Jefferson met up with him in New York and they set out on a tour through the lakes of upstate New York. They made it a bit past Crown Point in Essex County before they decided to turn back south toward a warmer clime, unaccustomed as the Virginia Piedmonters were to the cold temperatures and high winds of Lake Champlain in springtime.

The past two years had been eventful ones, with Madison the de facto leader of the House of Representatives and prime sponsor of the Bill of Rights. Not everything had unfolded as he had hoped, however. He was unsuccessful in his attempt to enact a policy of commercial discrimination against the British or in thwarting Secretary of the Treasury Alexander Hamilton's economic plan to assume the state debts and pay only the present holders of national bonds. But Madison himself had decided to forgo pushing his own policy on assumption in order to gain Hamilton's political assistance in locating the new capital on the Potomac – in Madison's home state and as far away from the stock jobbers in New York City as possible.[3] The start-up of the new government was an exhilarating but also an anxious time for the men who would shape the contours of the fledgling republic. Virtually all agreed that the major task at hand was to put political flesh on the frame of the Constitution and to "cement the union." In addition to the disaffected "Antifederalists," some of whom were still rather grudging in their acceptance of the wholesale revisions to the Articles of Confederation, the "friends of the Constitution" – who had agreed to the constitutional outline but not a specific legislative agenda – now faced the hard but less exalted and often divisive work of everyday policy formulation.

Toward the close of the First Congress, Alexander Hamilton unveiled his plan to establish a national bank. Within a short time after the bill's introduction, Madison stood on the floor of the House of Representatives to argue against it on the grounds that it violated the intended meaning of the Constitution (not to mention the Tenth Amendment of the Bill of

---

[3] For an excellent and provocative treatment of the reasons for Madison's intense concern about the location of the seat of the national government, see Drew R. McCoy, "James Madison and Visions of American Nationality in the Confederation Period: A Regional Perspective," in Richard Beeman, Stephen Botein, and Edward C. Carter II, eds., *Beyond Confederation: Origins of the Constitution and American National Identity* (Chapel Hill: University of North Carolina Press, 1987), 226–58.

Rights, which was less than two weeks short of becoming law of the land). In Madison's view, the attempt to establish a national bank marked a new level of political fissure in the nascent republic. It was not only sectional rivalries that would need to be assuaged and differences on policy questions that would require delicate compromise at the outset of the new government. Now the meaning of American constitutionalism and the character of republican government seemed to be at issue. Hamilton's proposed measure for the bank, combined with his apparent desire to perpetuate the national debt and encourage the speculators who rushed to take part in his enterprise, would create a class of wealthy citizens who possessed an undue influence on government, much as the way the British government operated. Madison was absolutely convinced – and had been for some time – that the British political system was not the model for America. Nonetheless, Hamilton's efforts to move the nation in the direction of the British model had received support from a majority of the members of Congress.

Vice President John Adams's labors threatened to move public opinion in a similar direction that, Madison believed, was incompatible with republicanism. Just weeks into the first administration, Adams proposed the use of British-style titles in America "with great *earnestness*," Madison complained.[4] Most recently, he had added a fourth volume to his *Defence of the Constitutions of Government of the United States of America*, titled *Discourses on Davila*, which was published in periodic installments in Fenno's *Gazette of the United States* in 1790–91. Madison, who regularly subscribed to the newspaper, had to ingest Adams's aristocratic views and "obnoxious principles" with his morning tea.

Hamilton's and Adams's admiration for the aristocratic British model of government was not news to Madison in 1791. In 1787 Hamilton had stood on the floor of the Constitutional Convention and remarked that in his "private opinion" he considered the British government to be the best in the world and doubted whether anything short of it would secure good government in America.[5] Madison had listened to and recorded this day-long brazen speech favoring an executive and a Senate for life, just as he noted Hamilton's endorsement of the British practice of "influence" and "corruption" in government.[6] Perhaps all of this would have been forgotten

---

[4] *PJM* 12:182.

[5] James Madison's version of Alexander Hamilton's "Speech on a Plan of Government," June 18, 1787, *PAH* IV:192. Cf. Alexander Hamilton's notes, IV:184; Robert Yates's version, IV:200; John Lansing's version, IV:204; Rufus King's version, IV:207.

[6] Adrienne Koch, ed., *James Madison's Notes of Debates in the Federal Convention of 1787* (Athens: Ohio University Press, 1966), 131–32, 175.

or chalked up to savvy political maneuvering had not Hamilton's public deeds and unguarded words later revealed otherwise. At the legendary dinner party hosted by Jefferson and attended by John Adams and Alexander Hamilton in April 1791, Hamilton once again demonstrated how audacious he could be. In response to Adams's pedantic remarks on the near perfection of the British constitution, which, he said, needed only to be purged of its corruption and equality of representation established in its popular branch, Hamilton's riposte must have tested the bounds of his host's civility: "Purge it of its corruption, and give to its popular branch equality of representation," Hamilton purportedly said, "and it would become an *impracticable* government: as it stands at present, with all its supposed defects, it is the most perfect government which ever existed."[7] Almost certainly Jefferson's good Madeira was flowing at the table that spring evening, and just as surely Jefferson repeated Hamilton's provocative remarks to his friend Madison the next time they talked.

At about the same time that Hamilton delivered his speech favoring a high-toned government at the Constitutional Convention, the first volume of Adams's *Defence* reached America. This text examined the strengths and weaknesses of republics, ancient and modern, and argued that the tripartite balanced constitution of Great Britain was the most excellent of models. Madison was quick to criticize the work. Though it has some merit, he wrote Jefferson, much of it is "unfriendly to republicanism." "Mr. Adams's Book . . . has excited a good deal of attention" and would probably "revive the predilections of this Country for the British Constitution."[8] "Men of learning find nothing new in it. Men of taste many things to criticize." It would nonetheless be read and praised "and become a powerful engine in forming the public opinion," he lamented. By the close of the First Congress, Madison had grown increasingly anxious about the influence of Adams's ideas on the American mind and future course of republicanism. During the course of that spring, he let loose his feeling about Adams's views in a private letter to Jefferson. Adams's work was "a mock defence of the Republican Constitutions of this Country," which he actually attacked with "all the force he possessed." To make matters worse, he composed and published his first volumes of the series while he was an official representative of the United States at a foreign court, and since becoming vice president, "his pen has been constantly at work in the same cause."[9]

---

[7] Adrienne Koch and William Peden, eds., *The Life and Selected Writings of Thomas Jefferson* (New York: Modern Library, 1972), 126.

[8] *PJM* 10:29.

[9] *PJM* 14:22.

After dining with Jefferson on March 13, and feeling reinvigorated by the fresh country air and companionable society, Madison returned to his lodgings at Mrs. House's Boarding House. With his books and papers spread about him in the small room he considered home in Philadelphia (he had stayed at Mrs. House's while a member of Congress in the early 1780s and during the Constitutional Convention as well), and with little clear space for sleeping anyway, he likely picked up the volume that lay open on his desk and resumed the "little task" he had set for himself that spring. His task centered on a study of Jean Jacques Barthélemy's *Voyage du jeune Anacharsis en Grèce dans le Milieu du Quatrième Siècle avant l'ère vulgaire*, a scholarly narrative that explores the culture and politics of classical Greece during the golden age.[10] One imagines Madison with the *Voyage* in one hand and a pen in the other, moving back and forth over twenty-two centuries in his mind. Adams had missed the central point of the classics' teaching on politics, Madison thought. The ancients certainly did *not* believe that republics could be sustained simply or even primarily by constructing an equilibrium in government, as if politics were essentially a balance scale of weights and pulleys. The vice president's "extravagant self importance"[11] and scholarly pretensions would do greater harm to the country than he knows and certainly more than Mr. Jefferson realizes, Madison mused.

Madison undoubtedly worked late into many a night in the spring of 1791, reading until his eyes grew weary and his back sore, learning as much as he could from "the great oracles of political wisdom." Sometimes, too, he picked a fight with these oracles, or with Adams and Hamilton, in his mind. Over the next year his scholarly endeavors would be left behind, replaced by more and more political and partisan activity, and finally by engagement in open party warfare. With Adams's public reputation on the wane, due particularly to the publication of *Discourses on Davila* and the *Publicola* essays (whose authorship was initially attributed to him rather than to his son, John Quincy) and the rising dominance of Hamilton in the Washington administration, Madison increasingly targeted his strategy of oppositional politics against the measures of the secretary of the treasury, though at least one of his later anonymously published essays was aimed at Adams. By the end of 1791, with an advance copy of Hamilton's "Report on Manufactures" in hand, Madison concluded that his worst fears had been realized. Hamilton meant, by administrative fiat, to undermine the Constitution as ratified and adopted by the American people and to alter the substance, and perhaps the form, of American republicanism. From Madison's perspective, Hamilton's

---

[10] *Voyage*, 5:62, 225.
[11] *PJM* 11:296.

funding system, the national bank, and governmental support of manufacturing were linked together in a clever scheme that mimicked the British financial system and, if successful, would increase the powers of the national government and establish a powerful and influential monied class in America. The "Report on Manufactures" revealed to Madison that Hamilton intended nothing less than the transformation of the economic and political life of America. By the spring of 1792, an open split between Federalists and the newly formed Republican Party was evident in America, with Alexander Hamilton at the helm of one party and James Madison the leading voice of the other.

Beginning in October 1791 and continuing through December of the following year, Madison published a series of nineteen unsigned articles, or Party Press Essays, in the newly launched Philadelphia newspaper the *National Gazette*. He and Jefferson had recruited Madison's old Princeton classmate, Philip Freneau, to establish the newspaper and serve as its editor, and Jefferson had offered Freneau part-time employment as a translator at the State Department in order to ease his financial condition (for which he would be accused of patronage by the Federalists). The objective of the *National Gazette* was to circulate republican ideas on the issues of the day and to counteract the effects of the systematically pro-administration newspaper, the *Gazette of the United States*. In chronological order of publication, Madison's articles in the *National Gazette* appeared as follows:

1. "Population and Emigration"
2. "Consolidation"
3. "Dependent Territories"
4. "Money" (Part I)
5. "Money" (Part II)
6. "Public Opinion"
7. "Government"
8. "Charters"
9. "Parties"
10. "British Government"
11. "Universal Peace"
12. "Government of the United States"
13. "Spirit of Governments"
14. "Republican Distribution of Citizens"
15. "Fashion"
16. "Property"
17. "The Union: Who Are Its Real Friends?"

18. "A Candid State of Parties"
19. "Who Are the Best Keepers of the People's Liberties?"

Unlike the "Notes on Government," upon which Madison based some but not most of the essays, there is no systematic order to the Party Press Essays, nor are they situated within the broad and enduring questions of political philosophy that characterized the "Notes." While they do incorporate important aspects of Madison's theoretical analysis of republicanism, the published essays in the *National Gazette* are primarily occasional pieces intended to address the political issues of the day. The essays can be divided roughly into two main categories: (1) those that emphasize the theoretical foundations of republicanism, and especially the centrality of the role of public opinion in free governments, and (2) those that focus on Republican opposition to certain economic and political policies of the Federalist administration. The former articles tend to be derivative of the philosophical arguments in the outline "Notes"; the latter have a much more partisan flavor that is not present in the "Notes."[12] The political pitch of the essays increases and intensifies over the period of publication; the tone of the first few essays, in fact, appears partisan only when viewed retrospectively, after a clear split between Federalists and Republicans became evident. Nonetheless, the initial essays do contain the seeds of what would become matters of acute party dispute. In rough outline, the transformation of the "republican cause" into the Republican Party can be traced by following Madison's rhetoric through the Party Press Essays of 1791–92.

Although Madison never mentioned Adams or Hamilton by name in these essays, he nonetheless implicated the former's alleged defense of republican government and the latter's role in initiating measures such as the funding system, the national bank, and governmental support of manufactures in the trend toward monarchy or aristocracy in America. Whether Hamilton or Adams actually sought to establish hereditary distinctions in America was not the central issue – though some Federalists probably did, and Madison believed that Adams's publications and the treasury secretary's financial program played into their schemes, providing the impetus toward new-modeling the American government on the British system. Their views and measures

---

[12] The general role of public opinion is taken up in five of the essays, viz., "Public Opinion," "Parties," "British Government," "Spirit of Governments," and "Who Are the Best Keepers of the People's Liberties?" Madison further explored the critical significance of the federal principle to the politics of public opinion in four of the Essays, namely, "Consolidation," "Government," "Charters," and "Government of the United States." The remaining essays deal with issues respecting public policy choices in the first administration, and primarily concern domestic and foreign fiscal policies of the Federalists, though some of these combine practical policy issues with theoretical considerations.

were "more accommodated to the depraved examples" of monarchy and aristocracy than to the genius of republicanism and, whether intended or not, might well "smooth the way to hereditary government" in America.[13] In contrast to Jefferson's accusations of monarchism leveled against Hamilton, Madison's implicit attacks in the Party Press Essays are more circumspect; they are couched in terms of the *impetus* or *tendency* of Federalist measures toward the establishment of a British-style system in the United States.

Madison believed that Adams sought to reproduce the equilibrium of the British model, if not by the creation of hereditary class distinctions, then by a mimetic equivalent of societal orders that would provide additional checks and balances in government, thereby presumably enhancing the stability of the political order.[14] Arguing that parties are inevitable in all governments, Adams claimed that "the great secret is to control them," either by instituting a monarchy and a permanent army or by establishing a balanced constitution. Adams clearly opted for the latter, calling for the institution of "standing powers" in order to avoid "greater evils."[15] This is a perverse understanding of the republican solution to the problem of parties, Madison argued in "Parties" – obliquely aiming his ink at Adams's published views. Since parties exist naturally in all political societies, legislators and statesmen must find ways to alleviate their baneful effects. The art lies in preventing or accommodating parties, to the extent possible, and when not possible, making them mutual checks upon one another. By contrast, the notion of adding "more scales and... more weights to perfect and maintain the equilibrium," that is, by promoting the creation of new parties or strengthening existing ones in order to achieve additional mutual checks in society, Madison declared, is "absurd." Though this is the theory that undergirds the use of artificial distinctions such as king, nobles, and plebeians to attain a balanced government, it is simply not the republican way. It is analogous to the foolish ethicist who promotes new vices in order to counteract existing ones, and it "is as little the voice of reason, as it is that of republicanism."[16]

Madison further pursued the faulty analysis that he believed underscored the Federalists' praise of the British model with his direct critique of it in the essay "British Government."[17] In light of the praise lavished on it by men

---

[13] "The Union: Who Are Its Real Friends?" *PJM* 14:274.

[14] "Parties," *PJM* 14:197–98.

[15] Adams, *Defence of the Constitutions of Government of the United States,* vol. 3, *WJA* 6:118; 587–88.

[16] "Parties," *PJM* 14:198.

[17] "British Government," *PJM* 14:201–2. Cf. Madison's implicit criticism of the British model of government in "Spirit of Governments," *PJM* 14:233–34, and in *Federalist* 14. Despite

such as Hamilton and Adams, and with the views expressed by Adams in the *Defence* clearly in mind, Madison argued that the "boasted equilibrium" of the British government, so far as it is even true, is not primarily due to "the form in which its powers are distributed and balanced."[18] The stability of the British government "is maintained less by the distribution of its powers, than by the force of public opinion."[19] Stability and liberty are not secured by limiting the share of the people to a third of government and counteracting their influence by "two grand hereditary orders" with rival and hostile "feelings, habits, interests, and prerogatives," or by any simulation of the British model of class warfare or party contestation.[20]

Madison believed Hamilton intended his economic plan to invest the national government with "influence," thereby enabling it to dispense money and emoluments and strengthen its position vis-à-vis the states.[21] This was supported by the institution of a funding system, which would continue to provide the source for political influence as long as the debt was perpetuated – and he suspected that Hamilton intended to fund the debt in perpetuity.[22] Instead of setting a time for the redemption of the debt and making adequate provision to pay it off, which would lower inflation and reestablish public credit, Hamilton sought to finance the debt through increased borrowing. The two-part essay entitled "Money," which Madison published in 1791 but probably wrote in 1779–80 when he was a delegate to the Continental Congress, served as a response to the treasury secretary's funding scheme.[23] The two essays criticized the idea that an increased supply of active (paper) money would stimulate the economy, establish public credit, and increase productivity, thereby diminishing the debt and increasing the wealth of the nation. Madison did not believe that the value of money is

Madison's clear rejection of the British constitution as the model for America, Michael Zuckert claims that "a modern American form of republicanism, modeled on the British constitution [was] developed by [Jefferson's] friend, James Madison . . . and embodied more or less in the Constitution of the federal union" (Zuckert, *The Natural Rights Republic: Studies in the Foundation of the American Political Tradition* [Notre Dame, Ind.: University of Notre Dame Press, 1996], 221).

[18] "British Government," *PJM* 14:202.
[19] Ibid.
[20] "Who Are the Best Keepers of the People's Liberties?" *PJM* 14:427.
[21] Ibid.; "A Candid State of Parties," 14:371; "Spirit of Governments," 14:233.
[22] *PJM* 13:106, 317. Cf. *PJM* 15:474, 14:208, 274–75; James Madison to Edmund Randolph, March 14, 1790, *PJM* 13:106; Frederick Augustus Muhlenberg, "Address of the House of Representatives to the President," December 10, 1790, 13:317; James Madison to Thomas Jefferson, February 15, 1795, *PJM* 15:474; "Universal Peace," 14:208; "The Union: Who Are Its Real Friends?" 14:274–75.
[23] See *PJM* 1:309–10, n. 1.

regulated by the quantity in circulation. It depends instead on the credit of
the nation that issues it and on the time of its redemption to gold and silver.
Further, the value of gold and silver depends on the proportion of those
metals that a country possesses in relation to other commercial nations.

Funding schemes may or may not assist in the establishment of public
credit, Madison argued. If such a scheme is not carefully implemented,
demand-pull inflation may result, further increasing distrust of public credit
and leading to national bankruptcy. A cautiously executed funding program
can do no more than show the good faith of the nation and buy time in
which to increase its actual wealth, for funding itself does not increase the
wealth of a nation. At best, bills of credit only delay payment, and loan-office
certificates (which are redeemable only at future dates) actually increase the
national debt by adding to it the cost of exchange, reexchange, and accrued
interest. This creates an even greater need to relieve public credit. "In order
to relieve public credit sinking under the weight of an enormous debt,"
Madison sardonically wrote,

we invent new expenditures. In order to raise the value of our money, which depends
on the time of its redemption, we have recourse to a measure which removes its
redemption to a more distant day. Instead of paying off the capital to the public
creditors, we give them an enormous interest to change the name of the bit of paper
which expresses the sum due to them; and think it a piece of dexterity in finance, by
emitting loan-office certificates, to elude the necessity of *emitting bills of credit.*[24]

"No expedient could perhaps have been devised more preposterous and
unlucky," Madison declared.

Madison regarded the establishment of a national bank as an unconstitutional usurpation of power by the national government, believing it to be
neither *necessary* nor *proper* according to the Constitution, though he fully
recognized that it was a necessary element of Hamilton's scheme to fund the
debt and establish a class of wealthy industrialists who would wield political power in America. Taken together, the national bank and the funded
public debt encouraged a "spirit of speculation" within and without government.[25] Hamilton's system of public finance appealed to the avidity of
public officials, tempting them to substitute the motive of private interest
for public duty.[26] It directed governmental measures to the interest of the
few, providing the "monied men" with irresistible opportunities for further
enrichment.[27]

---

[24] *PJM* 1:309.
[25] "The Union: Who Are Its Real Friends?" *PJM* 14:274.
[26] "Spirit of Governments," *PJM* 14:233.
[27] "A Candid State of Parties," *PJM* 14:371.

In "Property," "Fashion," and "Republican Distribution of Citizens" Madison took implicit aim at Hamilton's "Report on Manufactures" and governmental schemes that favored one branch of industry over another rather than allowed the economy to follow its natural course. The wealth accumulated by the frenzy of speculative activity prompted by Hamilton's funding plan was to be channeled into the manufacturing industry, again by an unconstitutional exercise of power. Governmental manipulation of the choice of occupations via the artificial encouragement of manufactures would promote the interest of this class at the expense of other interests in the society, particularly the agricultural interest. Landholders would be burdened with arbitrary taxes while rich merchants were granted new and "*unnecessary* opportunities" to capitalize on their wealth.[28]

This show of partiality to the wealthy few, though touted as advancing the prosperity and happiness of the nation as a whole, would in time, Madison argued, actually give "such a turn to the administration, [that] the government itself may by degree be narrowed into fewer hands, and approximated to an hereditary form."[29] Designed to simulate the practices of the British system, it would introduce corruption and venality into government and encourage self-interest as its driving force. Madison contemptuously described this governmental model in "Spirit of Governments," arguing that such a government operates on the basis of "corrupt influence" and "private interest," rewarding the avidity of a part rather than benefiting the whole and supporting the domination of the few over a pretended liberty of the many.[30] Despite Montesquieu's, Hamilton's, and Adams's categorization of this type of government as a republic, Madison argued that in reality it is "an imposter." Fortunately, such a government was not yet established in America. It is to the honor of Americans that they never stoop to "mimic the costly pageantry of its form, nor betray themselves into the venal spirit of its administration."[31] In essence, Madison all but said, the Federalist admiration of the English model is in truth the approbation of corruption and aristocratic pomp. He did not say, though he may have thought it, that Hamilton was especially to blame for attempting to incorporate into America the British "venal spirit" of corruption and Adams for covetously endeavoring to copy "the costly pageantry" of the British monarchy.

[28] "Parties," *PJM* 14:197.
[29] "A Candid State of Parties," *PJM* 14:371.
[30] "Spirit of Governments," *PJM* 14:233.
[31] Ibid., 14:233–34.

By advancing the cause of speculators and manufacturers, Hamilton's plan would increase the dependence and servility of the common citizens, whose labor and livelihood would be captive to the fashionable tastes of the wealthy for luxury goods produced in the new industries. Economic dependency begets political dependency, Madison argued in "Property"; it has a deleterious effect upon liberty and strips the citizen of a sense of security in his person, his possessions, his faculties, and his opinions. Servility among American citizens at home would thus imitate the economic servility of America abroad. The lack of commercial reciprocity between the United States and Great Britain was for many years a particularly sore spot for Madison. Madison's first Party Press Essay, "Population and Emigration," published on November 19, 1791, and his second, "Dependent Territories," which appeared less than a month later, are both advocacy pieces for commercial discrimination against the British. Since the First Congress, Madison had labored diligently but unsuccessfully to enact a policy that would tax the goods and carrying ships of those countries that did not have economic treaties with the United States (i.e., Great Britain), thereby achieving commercial reciprocity or at least more advantageous commercial relations. In so doing, Madison sought to "discriminate" against America's former "mother country," thus following through on Publius's (Hamilton's) passionate call for a union strong enough to institute prohibitory trade regulations against Great Britain – indeed, for one powerful enough "to dictate the terms of the [economic] connection between the old and the new world!"[32] It was probably not an accident that Madison's articles on British commercial policy appeared just shortly after the first British minister plenipotentiary to the United States, George Hammond, arrived in Philadelphia to conduct negotiations pertaining to economic relations between the two countries.

In "Population and Emigration" Madison claimed that in respect to American exports to Great Britain, the United States is in possession of only about one-fifth of the carrying freight, even though it is actually entitled to half. America should not stand for Britain's "monopolizing" commercial policy, he argued, but should call for more just commercial relations between the two nations. Moreover, British emigration to the United States increases American demand for British products, British demand for raw materials from America, and cartage by British mariners and merchants,

---

[32] *Federalist* 11, passim. For an excellent study of Madison's and Hamilton's stances on U.S. commercial policy toward the British see Michael Schwarz, "The Great Divergence Reconsidered: Hamilton, Madison, and U.S.–British Relations, 1783–89," *Journal of the Early Republic* 27:3 (2007), 407–36.

thereby employing and sustaining a significant number of people in the British Isles who would otherwise lack the means of survival. In sum, British emigration to and trade with the United States are critical to Britain's prosperity. Why, he wanted to know, are we not demanding our fair commercial share?

In "Dependent Territories" Madison continued his criticism of Britain's policy of commercial discrimination, expanding it to include an attack on British colonialism. The British West Indies depended on the United States for the necessities of life, he argued, while Great Britain depended on us for the raw materials used in its manufacturing industry. Surely there is no reason to stand for the policy that American exports to the West Indies and England must be shipped in British bottoms (i.e., merchant vessels). In addition, the United States was Great Britain's best customer, while the former depended on the latter only for nonnecessities and luxury items. America could do without these or produce substitutes. Moreover, although Great Britain bought the bulk of American exports, it was not in actuality our best customer, for it reexported a significant amount of American produce to other countries, particularly France. The relationship of the West and East Indies to Great Britain is analogous to that between slave and master, Madison asserted, and it has a similar influence on the character of both. The master country cherishes "pride, luxury, and vanity," and the dependent territory learns "vice and servility, or hatred and revolt." This is precisely what happened in the case of the American Revolution, Madison implied, and our situation at present is little different from the financial dependence on Great Britain that we were forced to endure prior to political independence. Even under the new Constitution, the Federalists were unwilling to lay down the gauntlet, and the new nation's economic subordination to England was virtually unchanged since colonial times.

Madison's strong opposition to the policy of commercial nondiscrimination against the British in the 1790s was the leading, though not sole, cause of his sustained foreign policy battles with Hamilton and the Federalists throughout the decade and beyond. He saw Hamilton's hand clearly behind the president's Neutrality Proclamation of 1793, which declared the country's neutrality between England and France in the war that had broken out between them. Madison criticized the Proclamation both because he believed it was an executive usurpation of legislative authority and because sufficient consideration had not been given to the American-Franco Treaty of 1778. He suspected that the Proclamation was largely the result of Hamilton's unwarranted fear of British commercial retaliation if the United States upset the favorable balance of trade enjoyed by the former. To add insult to injury, Hamilton and the Federalists orchestrated the negotiation of a new treaty with Great Britain through the diplomatic aegis of John Jay in 1795, which they took pains to keep from the public eye until all was done and settled.[33] The new treaty, Madison believed, put America at an even greater economic disadvantage than it had been in previous years.

The war between England and France caused almost as much hostility between opposing camps in America as it did in Europe. Madison and Jefferson thought Hamilton and his cronies Anglophiles and mere toadies of the British government. Hamilton returned the compliment, calling Jefferson and Madison Francophiles whose attachment to France was "womanish." By the close of the decade, a pattern of missteps by the French minister Genêt and the heightened passions and suspicions of the French and their American defenders resulted in the passage of the Alien and Sedition Acts, which President John Adams somewhat reluctantly signed into law. Though Madison had left the capital scene in 1797 to return to his home at Montpelier with his new wife, Dolley, he was persuaded by Vice President Jefferson to once again put his pen to service in the Republican cause. Jefferson wrote the Kentucky Resolutions while Madison composed the Virginia Resolutions, calling upon the other states to join them in vehement opposition to measures that would destroy the sacred liberties of the American people. The Federalist assault on free speech, Madison argued, was part of their agenda to promote the submission of the people to the government. In republican government, he argued, "the censorial power is in the people over the government, and not in the government over the people."[34] Seeking to encourage "public confidence" rather than public watchfulness over the government, the Federalists would obstruct the institution that provides the channel to make the government of a large territory responsible to the people. They would suppress

---

33 See Todd Estes's insightful study of the politics surrounding the Jay Treaty in *The Jay Treaty Debate, Public Opinion, and the Evolution of Early American Culture* (Amherst: University of Massachusetts Press, 2006). According to Estes, "Some of the tactics and techniques used in the debate were not new, but their scale and deployment and effect on public opinion were.... [T]he Jay Treaty debate can be seen as the last vestige of an older, more deferential political culture championed by Federalists, even as the debate itself (and the tactics used by both sides) helped to hasten the acceptance of a more open, democratic culture espoused by the Republicans. In short, the Federalists won in the short term but found themselves losing the long-term struggle for control of the nation's political culture" (2–4).

34 "House Address to the President," November 27, 1794, *PJM* 15:391; cf. 11:163; James H. Read, *Power versus Liberty: Madison, Hamilton, Wilson, and Jefferson* (Charlottesville: University Press of Virginia, 2000), 69–70.

the free communication of opinions among the people, though this has ever been deemed "the only effectual guardian of every other right."[35]

Under Madison's initial leadership in 1791–92 the "republican cause" became the Republican Party. Throughout the 1790s Republicans united in opposition to the Federalist agenda, which they believed sought to dismiss or enervate the power of public opinion, distance the government from the will of the people, and undermine the people's spirit of independence and capacity for self-government. Whatever the differences between Adams's and Hamilton's visions for America, in this regard the Republicans viewed them as advancing the same antirepublican agenda.

Madison's central charge against the Federalists was that they denied the people the republican right to govern themselves. Believing that the people are "stupid, suspicious, [and] licentious," and that they cannot be trusted as keepers of their own liberties, the Federalists preached confidence in government and submission to its acts.[36] They appealed "less to the reason of the many than to their weaknesses" and have "debauched themselves into a persuasion that mankind are incapable of governing themselves." Republicans, on the other hand, believe that the people are "the best keepers of [their] liberties" and take offense "at every public measure that does not appeal to the understanding and to the general interest of the community, or that is not strictly conformable to the principles, and conducive to the preservation of republican government."[37] Rather than promote servile obedience to the government, they think that "the people ought to be enlightened, to be awakened, to be united, [and] that after establishing a government they should watch over it, as well as obey it."[38] In a word, they believe in "the doctrine that mankind are capable of governing themselves."[39]

Adams and Hamilton viewed matters from a very different and, they believed, more realistic perspective. Indeed, each saw himself as the rescuer of republicanism in a new age. For Adams, the challenge of republicanism was to provide an antidote to the pride of human nature, as it remained permanently in a fallen world, but that could now be controlled by a new conception of dynamic balances. For Hamilton, the solution lay in a new

---

35 Marvin Meyers, *The Mind of the Founder: Sources of Political Thought of James Madison* (Hanover, N.H.: Brandeis University Press, 1981), 262–63.
36 "Who Are the Best Keepers of the People's Liberties?" *PJM* 14:426–27.
37 "A Candid State of Parties," *PJM* 14:371.
38 "Who Are the Best Keepers of the People's Liberties?" *PJM* 14:426.
39 "A Candid State of Parties," *PJM* 14:371.

order of republicanism in the modern economic age of industry and competitive advantage. Madison thought Adams and Hamilton placed too much reliance on modern science and the mechanics of self-interest and did not attend sufficiently to the power of the human spirit. He too sought a new order of the ages, but one that he believed marked a more noble republican course.

2

The Federalist Agenda

Madison's philosophic lead in opposing the "antirepublican" views and measures of the early 1790s defined the essential controversy between what would soon become the first American political parties. But history does not always favor the victors, and Madison's characterization of his opponents as antirepublicans did not stick. To almost a man, the Federalists considered themselves the true proponents of republicanism, much as the Antifederalists of the 1780s believed themselves to be the real Federalists. The character of Federalist Party thought remains unsettled in scholarship today, with myriad books that criticize the views of men such as John Adams and Alexander Hamilton (generally from a "Jeffersonian perspective") and others that defend their republican credentials.[1] Despite the widely read and

[1] See Gordon Wood's analysis of Adams as a classical republican thinker in *The Creation of the American Republic, 1776–1787* (Chapel Hill: University of North Carolina Press, 1969), ch. 14. Robert Webking and John Patrick Diggins, in contrast, claim that Adams is more appropriately situated within the liberal tradition (*The American Revolution and the Politics of Liberty* [Baton Rouge: Louisiana State University Press, 1988]; *The Lost Soul of American Politics: Virtue, Self-Interest, and the Foundations of Liberalism* [New York: Basic Books, 1984]). In a sympathetic and thoughtful recent work on Adams, C. Bradley Thompson (*John Adams and the Spirit of Liberty* [Lawrence: University Press of Kansas, 2002]) defends Adams's republican credentials on the terms he himself set forth, rejecting the view of several leading scholars that identify him as a *classical* republican thinker. In fact, Thompson claims, Adams was "the first major American theorist to reject classical republicanism explicitly." Excellent studies on Hamilton's republican ideas include Gerald Stourzh, *Alexander Hamilton and the Idea of Republican Government* (Stanford, Calif.: Stanford University Press, 1970); Karl-Frederich Walling, *Republican Empire: Alexander Hamilton on War and Free Government* (Lawrence: University Press of Kansas, 1999); and Robert W. T. Martin, "Reforming Republicanism: Alexander Hamilton's Theory of Republican Citizenship and Press Liberty," in Douglas Ambrose and Robert W. T. Martin, eds., *The Many Faces of Alexander Hamilton: The Life and Legacy of America's Most Elusive Founding Father* (New York: New York University Press, 2006), 109–33. See also

influential essay by Daniel Rodgers, titled "Republicanism: The Career of a Concept," which proclaims the end of "republicanism" as a paradigm for the American Founding, such interpretive claims will no doubt continue in the literature on this era. This is as it should be, for the term "republican" is not a later invention by scholars that has been superimposed on the eighteenth century. Rather, it is a term employed regularly by the Founders themselves to describe a form of government whose origins date to classical times. That the word meant different things to different people is not a reason to abandon its usage. Instead, it is all the more reason to explore its meanings and to attempt to uncover the power of a concept that inspired men of such different views and that continues to define the nature of the American political system to this day.

Although historians have situated John Adams and Alexander Hamilton together under the banner of the Federalists, the union between them was precarious even in the best of times. Both considered themselves defenders of republicanism, both praised the British constitution of balanced government, and both believed that the version of republicanism that emerged from the Constitutional Convention was probably unworkable and that the United States would eventually have to move closer to the English model. Adams, however, did not share Hamilton's British-inspired vision of high finance and industrialization for America. Moreover, the personalities of the two men were decidedly unsuited to each other, and there was no love lost between them. Adams largely blamed Hamilton for his loss in the presidential election of 1800, though on this as on many other matters, he seems to have misread Hamilton.[2] Adams did not have Hamilton's analytical quickness of mind or his flair for risk, not to mention the New Yorker's good looks or charm. Dubbed "His Rotundity," Adams was stodgy in appearance and manner, and his mind tended toward the pedantic and plodding. His vanity and jealousy of others were well-known traits that many of his colleagues found irritating (including Madison), though they were offset by a remarkable fulsomeness of heart that marked his relationships with those he loved and

Ron Chernow, *Alexander Hamilton* (New York: Penguin Books, 2004); Stephen F. Knott, *Alexander Hamilton and the Persistence of Myth* (Lawrence: University Press of Kansas, 2002); John Lamberton Harper, *American Machiavelli: Alexander Hamilton and the Origins of U.S. Foreign Policy* (Cambridge: Cambridge University Press, 2004), 3–6. Cf. Gordon Wood's provocative and delightful compilation of articles on Hamilton and Adams (and other "worthies" of the Founding generation) in *Revolutionary Characters: What Made the Founders Different* (New York: Penguin Press, 2006).

[2] Forrest McDonald, Review of *The Papers of Alexander Hamilton*, Vols. XX–XXII, in *William and Mary Quarterly* 33:4 (1976), 678.

considered friends. Still, Adams was at times such a caricature of himself that his idiosyncrasies were irresistible fodder for anyone with a sense of satire. In fact, they still are. In the musical *1776* the puffed-up figure of Adams is, ironically, unforgettable. "I'll not be in the history books," Adams whines:

Only Franklin. Franklin did this, and Franklin did that, and Franklin did some other damn thing. Franklin smote the ground, and out sprang General Washington, fully grown and on his horse. Then Franklin electrified him with that miraculous lightning-rod of his, and the three of them – Franklin, Washington, and the horse – conducted the entire War for Independence all by themselves.

As perfectly wrought and comic as this little speech is, one might think that it is pure fiction. Actually, though, it is not far from what Adams actually did say, though the celebrity of the horse was high artistic invention. "The History of our Revolution will be one continued lye from one end to the other," Adams wrote Benjamin Rush in 1790. "The essence of the whole will be that Dr. Franklin's electric rod smote the earth and out sprang General Washington. Then Franklin electrified him . . . and thence forward those two conducted all the Policy, Negotiations, Legislations, and War."[3]

However foppish Adams may have been at times, no one doubted his sincere devotion to America or the significant contributions he made to the revolutionary cause. Next to Washington and Franklin, he was considered by his countrymen the leading senior statesman. He had been at the forefront of the American cause for independence since its inception, leading the way in the revolutionary war of ideas and in formulating constitutional structures for the new states. He chaired the committee that drafted the Declaration of Independence, authored *Thoughts on Government*, drafted the Massachusetts Constitution, and served as America's first minister to Great Britain under the new United States Constitution. With the publication of his four-volume *A Defence of the Constitutions of Government of the United States of America* in 1787–92, it was reasonable for Madison to expect that Adams's ideas would carry weight with the American people. Certainly Adams expected that they would.

The central thrust of the *Defence* is the case for the constitutional separation and balance of powers in government. It was aimed particularly at the views of the French politician and writer Anne Robert Jacques Turgot,

---

[3] Quoted in Robert Ferguson, "The American Enlightenment, 1750–1820" in Sacvan Bercovitch, ed., *Cambridge History of American Literature* (Cambridge: Cambridge University Press, 1994), 348.

who had criticized the American state constitutions' provisions for legislative bicameralism and checks and balances (Pennsylvania and Georgia, with their unicameral legislators, excepted), which Turgot asserted were imitations of the British royal government and had no place in a republic. The American states "endeavor to balance these powers," Turgot wrote,

as if this equilibrium, which in *England* may be a necessary check to the enormous influence of royalty, could be of any use in Republics founded upon the equality of all the Citizens, and as if establishing different orders of men, was not a source of divisions and disputes.[4]

In contrast to the English model, Turgot advocated that all authority be collected into "one center, the nation."[5] According to Adams, Turgot's scheme would concentrate all the powers of government – legislative, executive, and

---

[4] A. Turgot, "Letter from A. Turgot," in W. Bernard Peach and D. O. Thomas, eds., *The Correspondence of Richard Price*, 3 vols. (Durham, N.C.: Duke University Press, 1991), 2:13.

[5] Adams's critique is based on a letter Turgot sent to Dr. Richard Price in 1778, which Price published after Turgot's death in *Observations on the Importance of the American Revolution, and the Means of Making It a Benefit to the World* (Dublin: Printed for T. Cadell, in the Strand, 1785; repr., Whitefish, Mo.: Kessinger Publishing Company, 2007). It is interesting to note that John Adams's praise for mixed government in many ways paralleled that of Jean Louis Delolme, an intellectual adversary of Price. As David Lieberman argues in "The Mixed Constitution and the Common Law," in Mark Goldie and Robert Wokler, eds., *The Cambridge History of Eighteenth-Century Political Thought* (Cambridge: Cambridge University Press, 2006), 339: "In elucidating the history and operation of England's constitution, Delolme traversed well-rehearsed matters of political structures, government functions, and themes of balances and checks. Nonetheless, his study is indicative of how, by the mid-1770s, significantly divergent accounts had developed concerning the manner in which this government system produced its celebrated benefit: political liberty. The spectrum of interpretation can be indicated through a brief comparison of the sharply contrasting positions adopted in Delolme's tendentious rendering of England's separation of powers and in Richard Price's no less substantial recasting of England's mixed constitution in his 1776 *Observations on the Nature of Civil Liberty*. Ultimately, what divided the two theorists was a basic conflict over the nature of liberty, which by this time boasted a rich and distinguished pedigree. Price, who defined liberty in general with 'the idea of self-government or self-direction', identified civil freedom as the capacity of the members of a given community to govern and make laws for themselves" (Richard Price, *Observations on the Nature of Civil Liberty* in *Political Writings*, D. O. Thomas, ed. [Cambridge: Cambridge Texts in the History of Political Thought, [1776] 1991], 22, 23–24). Delolme (reacting here to the doctrines of Rousseau) directly repudiated this approach. "'To concur by one's suffrage in enacting laws' was to enjoy 'a share' of 'power'; 'to live in a state where the laws are equal . . . and sure to be executed' was 'to be free'" (Jean Louis DeLolme, *The Constitution of England; or, An Account of the English Government*, William Hughes, ed. [London, [1771] 1834], 212; and see William Paley, *Principles of Moral and Political Philosophy*, in *Works of William Paley*, Edmund Paley, ed., 4 vols, [London: [1785] 1838], 3:250–52).

judicial – in one representative assembly. Would Turgot have no checks, no orders, no balance, Adams asked in astonishment?

Adams's intention in writing the *Defence* was only partially to present a critique of Turgot's opposition to bicameralism and mixed, balanced government, however. That could have been done quite easily and in a brief exposition, he admitted. Adams's goal was also to assemble the views of the most thoughtful philosophers, historians, and politicians "whose writings were in the contemplation of those who framed the American constitutions."[6] The preservation and destruction of governments is a subject that engaged the attention of these writers whose influence may be seen in America, and their analysis shows "the utility and necessity of different *orders* of men, and an *equilibrium* of powers and privileges."[7]

Adams thought the classical idea of mixed, balanced government was best summarized by Polybius. He accepted Polybius's general premise of the need to institutionalize the rivalry between the different social classes within the government, but he believed he had improved on the classical doctrine by including three, rather than only two, opposing weights within the scale of government. To accomplish this, he blended the classical mixed government theory with the modern notion of separation of powers set forth by Montesquieu, thereby advancing the idea of a strong and independent executive and a tripartite separation of independent powers and balances within the legislative branch of government.[8] Though Adams did not advocate a balance of hereditary orders, he nonetheless sought to institute a system of class rivalry and counterpoises within government as imitative of the British model as possible. History shows that the classical republics that maintained themselves the longest were able to do so because they incorporated a balance of social orders and rivalries within their constitutional structures, he argued. Ultimately, however, their corruption and demise were due to their defective conception of a dual rather than tripartite balance, the latter of

---

[6] Adams, *Defence of the Constitution of Government of the United States*, vol. 2, WJA 4:435.

[7] Ibid., vol. 1, WJA 4:440.

[8] See David Wootton's in-depth discussion of the distinction between the theory of mixed and balanced government, on the one hand, and the separation of powers, on the other, in "Liberty, Metaphor, and Mechanism: The Origins of Modern Constitutionalism," in D. Womersley, ed., *Liberty and American Experience in the Eighteenth Century* (Indianapolis: Liberty Fund, 2006), 209–74. Wootton argues that it is necessary to understand this distinction in order to recognize the various and differing ways that the idea of checks and/or balance(s) has been conceived by writers on government. Adams attempted to bring together the diverse analytical and historical traditions associated with mixed government (and balance) and separation of powers (and checks). Prior to Adams, Spelman's translation of Polybius's fragment on the balanced constitution made "checks" and "balances" virtually equivalent.

which, in practice at least, was never accomplished prior to the establishment of the English constitution.[9]

It may seem ironic that the Founder who was perhaps hardest on himself (and his sons), in terms of living up to moral standards, did not make more of a place for virtue in his political philosophy. Undoubtedly, Adams considered virtue absolutely necessary to happiness and the good life.[10] But he also believed that human beings seldom choose virtue for virtue's sake, that in fact they tend to covet the sham virtue of honor or distinction, and that the wise legislator will arrange the operations of the various classes of society to counteract this fundamental fact of human nature. In Adams's mind, the institutionalization of social orders within government was not an endorsement of aristocracy but the recognition of the prideful nature of man and the need to control its harmful effects. He believed that the passion for distinction is present in every human soul, from the lowliest clerk to the blue-blooded aristocrat. In commercial societies, the desire for wealth (and the distinction it brings) moves the common man, and the institutionalization of this interest serves to check the ambitions of the few. Conversely, aristocratic pride, "which looks down on commerce and manufactures as degrading," especially when supported by "the pompous trumpery of ensigns, armorials, and escutcheons," can help to prevent "the whole nation from being entirely delivered up to the spirit of avarice" in commercial nations. According to Ralph Lerner, Adams considered such pretensions "mischievous and ridiculous in America," but nonetheless recognized that some sorts of countermeasures to "the universal gangrene of avarice" are necessary. He thus encouraged utilizing the rivalry between acquisitiveness and pride of birth to achieve a balance of passions and prejudices within the political order.[11]

In the third volume of the *Defence* Adams focused his attack on Marchamont Nedham, a seventeenth-century British writer considered a leading exponent of republican ideas.[12] Turgot's idea of collecting all authority

---

[9] Adams, *Defence*, vol. 1, WJA 4:469, 559.

[10] See Andrew S. Trees's discussion of Adams's views on the relative importance of virtue versus governmental arrangements in civic life in *The Founding Fathers and the Politics of Character* (Princeton, N.J.: Princeton University Press, 2003), 75–105.

[11] "Commerce and Character: The Anglo-American as New-Model Man," *William and Mary Quarterly* 36 (1979), 23 and n. 58.

[12] According to Paul Rahe, Marchamont Nedham did propagate republicanism and populism – but of the Machiavellian stripe (Paul A. Rahe, "Machiavelli in the English Revolution," in Rahe, ed., *Machiavelli's Liberal Republican Legacy* [Cambridge: Cambridge University Press, 2006], xxiii, 1–22). Rahe argues that Nedham's bow to man's rational capacities and to self-government was "no more than a passing rhetorical flourish, conferring a certain specious dignity on a populist argument that is otherwise Machiavellian through and

into "'one center,' and that center the nation," was probably derived from Nedham, Adams claimed.[13] Adams understood that Turgot meant by "the nation" the people. Subsequent to the original agreement to form the nation, however, Adams believed that to speak of the nation was euphemistic. At this stage, there really is no entity that can be properly termed the nation or the people, he argued; rather, there is the majority and the minority in a state. Nedham had set forth the fundamental principle that "the people . . . are the best keepers of their own liberties."[14] "But who are the people?" Adams asked. "If by *the people* is meant the whole body of a great nation," he responded,

it should never be forgotten, that they can never act, consult, or reason together, because they cannot march five hundred miles, nor spare the time, nor find a space to meet; and therefore, the proposition, that they are the best keepers of their own liberties, is not true. They are the worst conceivable; they are no keepers at all. They can neither act, judge, think, or will, as a body politic or corporation."[15]

If by the people is meant the majority, or the majority represented in successively chosen assemblies and responsible only to their constituents, without the check of an independent executive and senate composed of different orders of men, the proposition is also false. "The majority has eternally, and without one exception, usurped over the rights of the minority," Adams contended.[16] The English government is the only one that has provided against this problem and, indeed, is the only "scientifical government"; by

---

through" (13). Although it is beyond the scope of this project to pursue, Rahe has also noted in conversations with me that it is "odd that Adams thinks Nedham the inspiration of Turgot: Nedham was a very early proponent of the separation of powers." See also Rahe's discussion of Nedham in his forthcoming volume, *Soft Despotism, Democracy's Drift* (New Haven, Conn.: Yale University Press, 2008). Cf. Paul A. Rahe, *Republics Ancient and Modern: Classical Republicanism and the American Revolution* (Chapel Hill: University of North Carolina Press, 1992), 409–26; Blair Worden, "Marchamont Nedham and the Beginnings of English Republicanism, 1649–1656," in David Wootten, ed., *Republicanism, Liberty, and Commercial Society, 1649–1776* (Stanford, Calif.: Stanford University Press, 1994), 45–81; Blair Worden, "'Wit in a Roundhead': The Dilemma of Marchamont Nedham," in Susan D. Amussen and Mark A. Kishlansky, eds., *Political Culture and Cultural Politics in Early Modern England: Essays Presented to David Underdown* (Manchester, U.K.: Manchester University Press, 1995), 301–37; Blair Worden and Joad Raymond, "The Cracking of the Republican Spokes," *Prose Studies* 19 (1996), 255–74; Joseph Frank, *Cromwell's Press Agent: A Critical Biography of Marchamont Nedham, 1620–1678* (Lanham, Md.: University Press of America, 1980).

13 Adams, *Defence*, vol. 3, *WJA* 6:6.

14 Ibid.,

15 Ibid., *WJA* 6:6–7.

16 Ibid., *WJA* 6:10; 61; 127.

instituting "standing powers" based on the natural orders of men, it has avoided much "greater evils."[17]

In Madison's Party Press Essay "Who Are the Best Keepers of the People's Liberties?" a hypothetical "republican" defends the idea that the people are the best keepers of their own liberties. In response, a hypothetical "anti-republican" rejects this fundamental tenet, searching instead for "the mysteries of government" in the "science of the stars" and "fathoming the depths where truth lies hidden" and the "secret art" of government is to be found. "Wonderful as it may seem," the anti-republican says, "the more you increase the attractive force of power, the more you enlarge the sphere of liberty." In fact, the establishment of two grand orders "inveterately hostile to the rights and interests of the people" – "by a *mysterious* operation" – results in the fortification of their rights and interests. "Mysterious indeed!" the republican mockingly responds, "but mysteries belong to religion, not to government, to the ways of the Almighty, not to the works of man."

Madison's implicit target in this essay is Adams; his anti-republican mouthpiece echoes Adams's argument in the chapter on Benjamin Franklin in the first volume of the *Defence*. Citing the anecdote that Franklin supposedly told at the 1776 Pennsylvania Convention during the debate about whether there should be one or two legislative assemblies, Adams recounted Franklin's story about a group of wagoners. In order to descend a steep hill with a heavy load, the wagoners tied two cattle to the front of the wagon to pull it down the hill *and* two cattle to the back of the wagon to pull it up. The cattle in front, plus the weight of the load, overbalanced the pair pulling up the hill and the wagon moved "slowly and moderately down the hill."[18] Perhaps, Adams remarked, Franklin might have recalled from Newton that for every action there must be an equal and contrary reaction, or there can be no rest. Had Harrington been in attendance at the convention, Adams continued, he would have said, as he once did when remarking on two girls dividing a cake and choosing a piece, "O! the depth of the wisdom of God, which, in the simple invention of a carter, has revealed to mankind the whole mystery of a commonwealth." Or he might have mentioned the "centripetal and centrifugal forces by which the heavenly bodies are continued in their orbits, instead of rushing to the sun, or flying off in tangents among comets and fixed stars impelled or drawn by different forces in different directions, they are blessings to their own inhabitants. . . . "

[17] Ibid., *WJA* 6:118.
[18] Ibid., vol. 1, *WJA* 4:390; cf. 4:410–13.

In Franklin and Turgot's advocacy of one assembly, there is nothing to restrain it, Adams claimed. The jealousy and vigilance of the people will not serve as a check on their representations; this is a "mere delusion." There ought to be no jealousy between the electors and the elected. It is contradictory to think that at one moment the people should extend to their representative "affection" and "confidence" and at the next harbor a "suspicion" of him. Rather, the properly instituted assembly reflects the "unreserved confidence" of the "collective body of the people."

The notion of collecting all authority into one center, the nation, is a "charming" one in which "brothers... live in harmony!" Adams sarcastically concluded. "How many beautiful sentiments, in heavenly numbers, from writers sacred and profane, might be said or sung in honor of peace, concord, harmony and brotherly love!"[19] It is true that good republics are virtuous, but virtue is not the cause of good government; instead, it is the result of a well-ordered, scientific constitution. It may even be true that a republic can exist among "highwaymen" if the constitution sets one "rogue to watch another."[20]

Turgot's pupil, Condorcet, in *Lettres d'un bourgeois de New-Heaven* (as in New Haven, Connecticut, where Condorcet was an honorary member – the spelling undoubtedly an intentional error), took up his pen to refute Adams's attack on his teacher. Condorcet's *Lettres* were published in the first volume of Philip Mazzei's *Recherches historiques et politiques sur les États-Unis de l'Amérique septentrionale* in 1788. In 1793 Condorcet discussed in more depth some of the ideas he had set forth in earlier works, in his *Outlines of an Historical View of the Progress of the Human Mind*. When reading or rereading this work in later years, Adams, as was his wont, wrote comments in the margins of the pages. In response to Condorcet's remark that knowledge has become part of an energetic and universal commerce, and that a new kind of authority – public opinion – has been established, which exercises "a less tyrannical empire over the passions, but a more firm and lasting power over reason," Adams jotted in the margin of the page: "The public opinion is at times as great a tyrant as Marat."[21] To Condorcet's claim that a tribunal has been erected in favor of justice and reason, Adams remarked, "As often in favor of error, absurdity, and vice as of reason and

[19] Ibid., vol. 3, *WJA* 6:200.
[20] Ibid., vol. 3, *WJA* 6:219.
[21] Zoltán Haraszti, *John Adams and the Prophets of Progress* (Cambridge, Mass.: Harvard University Press, 1952), 251.

justice." In reaction to Condorcet's claim that a free press resists new errors from their birth, and that often they are attacked and eradicated even before they have spread, Adams acerbically wrote, "There has been more new error propagated by the press in the last ten years than in an hundred years before 1798." Adams went on to attack Marat and others, who, when they had in their hands the "empire of the press," were more tyrannical than Caesar Borgia. One wonders, though, given his mention of the date 1798 and the American controversy surrounding the Alien and Sedition Acts that he was embroiled in that year, whether he was thinking only of the French press.

Adams's disdain for what he considered the lunacy of French ideas was at a high point in the years leading up to and following the French Revolution. It was not, however, at its peak. When he later revised and added supplemental notes to his volumes of the *Defence* in 1813 (and with Napoleon in power), he hit a new acme of ridicule. The "mysterious science" that in the Party Press Essays Madison had mocked Adams for advocating now became the brunt of derision in an attack by Adams upon French "Ideology." "Ideology," or "that obscure metaphysics" that searches after "first causes" upon which to found the legislation of nations, he wrote, is a new word for which the literary and political worlds are deeply indebted. The English word "Idiocy" hardly expresses the power or meaning of the new science, though it may provide its proper definition. "And a very profound, abstruse, and mysterious science it is," Adams jeered. "It was taught in the school of folly, but alas, Franklin, Turgot, Rochefoucauld and Condorcet, under Tom Paine, were the great masters of that Academy!"[22]

Despite his sometimes piercing sarcasm, Adams's plodding mind and labored intellectual forays stand in rather droll contrast to Hamilton's razor-sharp analytical abilities and his often hastily written yet brilliant reports and essays. No one of the Founding generation could match Hamilton for quickness of mind or flashes of pure intellectual genius. Not even Madison, who studied and worked through questions with a thoroughness that the quick-witted Hamilton seldom mustered the patience to do. Hamilton was a natural; Madison was a scholar. Hamilton was not only graced with natural genius – he knew it. He carried himself with an air of self-possession that was the reflection of genuine pride and not mere vanity, though it was nonetheless often irksome to his colleagues. "The spectacle of a person who is certain he knows how to do almost anything better than everyone else is normally irritating," write Stanley Elkins and Eric McKitrick. "So it would be on more than one occasion with Alexander Hamilton. But most of the

---

[22] *Discourses on Davila* in Adams, *Defence*, vol. 4, *WJA* 6:402–3, n. B.

time such a trait in his case was not the defect it might have seemed in others, but a clear asset, since he generally *could* do it better."[23]

In the 1760s Alexander Hamilton was but an orphaned teenager working as a clerk at a trading post on the remote island of St. Croix. On many a clear Caribbean day, with only the vast ocean separating him from his aspirations, he looked north across the waters, dreaming of the country and the reputation that might someday be his. The images in his mind were not pipe dreams. The proprietor of the shop where he spent his days recognized the youth's intellectual abilities, and his ambition too. Hamilton would shortly travel to America and rise to the highest ranks of public service, leaving, ultimately, only presidential ambitions unfulfilled. Unlike Adams, Jefferson, or Madison, the young Hamilton saw Revolutionary War battle and undoubtedly heard the sound of bullets flying past his ear. Perhaps, like Washington, he too found something charming in the sound. In Washington's mind, there was no young man of more talent, principle, or daring than Hamilton. In everything but biology, he was the son Washington had always wanted. Hamilton loved Washington but did not always defer to him; he was as intent on becoming his own man and making a name for himself as he was on making America a great nation. "America is a Hercules," he once wrote, "but a Hercules in the cradle."[24]

Following the establishment of the new government in 1789 and his appointment to the post of secretary of the treasury, Hamilton consciously set about making the United States the greatest economic and political power on earth. While his contributions to American economic greatness may not, like his life in general, make for a saga of romantic proportions, the chronicle is nonetheless an amazing one. It is writ large on the annals of the country that took him in and raised him from boy to manhood. In turn, he adopted America as his own and reared it from a fledging nation to one that would soar in the economic and political skies for at least two centuries to come.

Hamilton's financial system consisted of three essential elements. First and foremost was the need to establish public credit in the United States. The initial step in accomplishing this was the establishment of an adequate system of funding the national debt. Whereas an unfunded debt is the object of excessive speculation, drains the nation of capital, and diverts funds from useful and productive industry, a properly instituted funding system supplies active capital in a country deficient in capital. Once public securities have

---

[23] Stanley Elkins and Eric McKitrick, *The Age of Federalism: The Early Republic, 1788–1800* (New York: Oxford University Press, 1993), 95.
[24] Hamilton to Washington, April 14, 1794, *PAH* 16:272.

acquired an adequate and stable value and the confidence of the community is established, the debt may serve as an engine of credit by promoting the transfer and exchange of funds. With additional capital in circulation, interest rates decrease; the stabilization of public stock moderates the spirit of speculation and directs capital to more useful channels. In Hamilton's view, the depreciated condition of landed property in America resulted from the scarcity of money. The increased quantity and circulation of capital would help to improve the state of agriculture. Further, it would unclog the wheels of commerce, thereby promoting commerce and manufacturing as well.[25] While Hamilton conceded that his program benefited the monied men of America, he denied that it created a special monied interest adverse to other citizens. Rather, he argued, investment in public stock promotes the economic growth of the nation, including all the useful industries in which the citizens are engaged. Productivity is increased and employment rises, further increasing the active and actual capital of a nation. Industry in general flourishes, "and herein," Hamilton declared, "consist[s] the true wealth of a nation."[26]

The second prong of Hamilton's financial program involved the establishment of a national system of banking that would fortify the establishment of public credit. The institution of a national bank was, in his opinion, more than an optional supplement to the funding system. Whereas banks are "*useful* in Countries greatly advanced in wealth," he argued, they are absolutely "*necessary* in Countries little advanced in wealth."[27] The advantages derived from a national bank include (1) augmentation of the active and productive capital of the nation, (2) greater ability of the government to obtain financial support, especially in times of emergency, and (3) assistance in the payment of taxes.[28] A national bank increases the supply of active capital by its ability to lend and circulate greater amounts of capital than the actual sum of its stock in coin. For all practical purposes, then, industry and trade would receive an absolute increase of capital infusion, and economic enterprise would be enlarged. In this way, banks are "the nurseries of national wealth."[29] Hamilton defended the constitutional authority of the national government to establish a national bank on the grounds that the

---

[25] Hamilton to Robert Morris, April 30, 1781, *PAH* 2:618.
[26] Ibid.
[27] "Notes on the Advantages of a National Bank," *PAH* 8:220.
[28] "Final Version of the Second Report on the Further Provision Necessary for Establishing Public Credit (Report on a National Bank)," *PAH* 7:306.
[29] Ibid.

right to erect corporations is inherent in the very definition of government. In defending the bank in a private letter to Washington, he couched his case in more practical terms: "[T]he most incorrigible theorist among [the bank's] opponents would in one month's experience as head of the Department of the Treasury be compelled to acknowle[d]ge that it is an absolutely indispensable engine in the management of the Finances, and would quickly become a convert to its perfect constitutionality."[30]

It was in response to the third prong of Hamilton's financial scheme that Madison mounted a full-scale opposition against his "antirepublican" program and, with his political allies, adopted the appellation "the republican party." Hamilton's "Report on Manufactures" was premised on the idea that the accelerated growth of manufacturing in the United States was essential to the national interest. The manufacturing industry, Hamilton argued, enhances the produce and revenue of the community, contributes to the diversification and division of labor, increases employment and productivity by engaging persons not ordinarily working, promotes foreign emigration, furnishes broader scope for the differing talents and dispositions of persons, increases the demand for agricultural produce, and makes the United States less dependent on foreign markets. Despite the clear and certain economic benefits that the growth of manufactures would produce in the nation, this does not guarantee that it will naturally occur, or occur as quickly as the country requires. Human beings are creatures of habit and tend to adopt untried industries reluctantly and slowly. "To produce the desirable changes, as early as may be expedient," he said, "may therefore require the incitement and patronage of government."[31] The supply of active capital needed to encourage manufacturing in the new republic was already in place via the funded debt and the national bank. Speculation in public stocks could thus be directed to useful purposes and away from its sometimes pernicious effects. Although the encouragement of manufactures in America would be disadvantageous to the other classes of society and to consumers in the short term, Hamilton argued that the long-term permanent effect would be to the benefit of all classes of society and the nation as a whole.

Hamilton's economic program was designed to stabilize the fiscal situation of the country, stimulate productivity, and set America on the course of prodigious material prosperity. His intent was to establish the economic foundation on which political stability and greatness depended. He had no

---

[30] Hamilton to Washington, August 18, 1792, *PAH* 12:251.
[31] "Alexander Hamilton's Final Version of the Report on the Subject of Manufactures," *PAH* 10:267.

wish, he repeatedly claimed, to establish monarchy or aristocracy in America or to introduce hereditary distinctions of any kind. That he was bent on corrupting a portion of the legislature he pronounced false and malignant. He rebuffed the charge that he was attempting to overturn the state governments or pervert limited government; there is a good deal of ambiguous ground concerning the demarcation between the general and the state governments over which honest men might disagree, he asserted. Finally, he flatly denied that he and the Federalists were conspiring to overthrow republican government in the United States, or even that their measures would *tend* to subvert the republican form or *prepare the way for* monarchy.[32] In exasperation Hamilton could only ask in regard to his opponents' accusations: When ever were "men more ingenious to torment themselves with phantoms?"[33]

Hamilton intended his economic blueprint for America to achieve both individual security and national strength. His conception of the connection between political stability and economic prosperity was presented most explicitly in his daylong speech of June 18 at the Constitutional Convention. In societies where industry is encouraged, Hamilton argued, individual security is often threatened by the clash of the distinct and rival interests between the few and the many, that is, between the wealthy, well-born, educated citizens and the mass of the people. If either group has all the power, it will oppress the other. "Both therefore ought to have power that each may defend itself agst. the other."[34] Moreover, given the "violence & turbulence" of the democratic spirit, it is particularly crucial to establish a separate and permanent body to check the unsteadiness and imprudence of the mass of the people.[35] The principle of representation is not sufficient to resist "the popular current," for the most popular branch of the legislature will predominate, and within it a few individuals tend to prevail.[36] Dependent on the favor of the people for the continuation of their position and power, these leaders often sacrifice the permanent interest of the nation to the passionate and partial interests of the many.

---

[32] Hamilton to Washington, August 18, 1792, *PAH* 12:248–53; cf. Washington to Hamilton, July 29, 1792, *PAH* 12:131–33.

[33] Hamilton to Adams, August 16, 1792, *PAH* 12:209.

[34] James Madison's version of Alexander Hamilton's "Speech on a Plan of Government," June 18, 1787, *PAH* 4:192.

[35] Alexander Hamilton's notes for "Speech on a Plan of Government," June 18, 1787, *PAH* 4:185; James Madison's version of Alexander Hamilton's "Speech on a Plan of Government," 4:193; Robert Yate's version, 4:200; John Lansing's version, 4:204.

[36] Alexander Hamilton's notes for "Speech on a Plan of Government," June 18, 1787, *PAH* 4:185.

The problem of the force of majority faction is therefore not solved by the representative principle. Nor, Hamilton contended, is the difficulty overcome by the establishment of a government over a large extent of territory, as Madison seemed to suppose. Although representatives chosen from larger districts may be of some benefit, frequently a small portion of a large district carries an election.[37] The representatives of an extensive nation still meet in one room and are liable to the same influences as those in a small country, including the charm of a powerful demagogue. In addition, the deterrent effect of the size of a nation on the formation of a majority faction is of doubtful veracity; combinations of a majority on the basis of interest will not be as difficult or unlikely as is assumed. Geographical and economic factors can and will influence the people and their representatives, and "it is easy to conceive a popular sentiment pervading" one portion, even a major portion, of the legislature.[38] In essence, Madison's analysis of the problem of majority faction and his proffered solution of the extended republic and representation, which he presented on June 6 on the Convention floor and later summarized in the 10th *Federalist*, was inadequate to the task of remedying the defects of popular government. In Hamilton's view, Madison's proffered solution was not a well-thought-through solution to the problem at all.

Hamilton contended that the problem of majority tyranny necessitates the establishment of a "permanent barrier" in government that would counteract the passionate demands of the many, particularly their covetousness toward the property of others.[39] The British provided for this barrier in their House of Lords. Hamilton believed that an equally effectual check on the turbulent and changing multitude was needed in America. Accordingly, he proposed a senate for life or during good behavior, arguing that the seven-year senate term supported by some delegates, including James Madison, was not sufficient for the purpose.[40] But just as there ought not to be too much dependence on popular sentiments, there ought not to be too little.[41] Hamilton recommended a House of Representatives of enlarged numbers, elected directly by the people every three years. The two branches of the legislature would balance each other in terms of the many versus the

---

[37] "Notes Taken in the Federal Convention," *PAH* 4:166.

[38] Ibid., *PAH* 4:165.

[39] James Madison's version of Alexander Hamilton's "Speech on a Plan of Government," June 18, 1787, *PAH* 4:192.

[40] See the discussion regarding the Senate of Maryland throughout the Convention debates.

[41] "Remarks in Support of a Three-Year Term for Members of the House of Representatives," *PAH* 4:214.

few, turbulence versus inertia, and protection of equal rights versus security for property rights. One chamber would manifest the "sensibility" of the populace, the other "knowledge and firmness" in public affairs.[42] It would be a kind of balance and the "happiest mode of conciliating" contraries, anticipating Jane Austen's felicitous equipoise of *Sense and Sensibility*.

The two-weighted scale protects the few and the many from oppression by each other, thereby contributing to the security of individual rights. But Hamilton thought more than this was needed. Like Adams, he advocated adding a third weight to the scale in the form of a single elected executive serving for life or good behavior. The executive would possess an absolute negative on legislation and, in turn, would himself be subject to counterbalancing checks by the legislature. Accordingly, the executive would provide an additional check against the passage of laws based on partial interest. In positive terms, Hamilton's executive was to serve as the dominant active agency in government. Characterized by unity, duration, and energy, his ambitions would be virtually one with the interests of the nation. He would move government to act with vigor, dispatch, and regularity, providing a sense of national character, strength, and permanency of will. An independent judiciary would supplement the checks against the legislature and its natural tendency to dominate in popular governments. This check on legislative power would further increase the proportionate authority of the republican executive.

Hamilton's central objective in his June 18 speech was to demonstrate the need for a "permanent *will*" in the government.[43] His plan was partly modeled on the British constitution, particularly in regard to the separation of powers based on two distinct interests in society and an energetic executive who would embody the interest of the nation as a whole. However, unlike the monarchic model, Hamilton claimed that his plan was fully consistent with the principles of republicanism: in it "the Executive and Legislative organs are appointed by a popular Election, and hold their offices upon a responsible and defeasible tenure."[44] Granted, subsequent to (indirect) election by the people, the Senate and executive would be as far removed from popular will as republican principles would allow. A democratic assembly cannot be properly checked by a democratic Senate, nor a democratic legislature by

---

[42] "New York Ratifying Convention: First Speech of June 25 (Francis Child's version)," *PAH* 5:81.

[43] Alexander Hamilton's notes for "Speech on a Plan of Government," June 18, 1787, *PAH* 4:186.

[44] "To the *New York Evening Post*," February 24, 1802, *PAH* 25:537.

a democratic executive, Hamilton argued.[45] Gouverneur Morris described the problem in earthier tones:

[T]he members of both Houses are creatures which, though differently born, are begotten in the same way and by the same sire. . . . The President can . . . do what he pleases, provided it shall always please him to please those who lead a majority of the Representatives.[46]

Hamilton urged his colleagues to see that the only effectual method to secure the ends of republican government was to overcome the contest between the few and the many. Like a host of renowned thinkers before him, Hamilton saw in the British constitution a model that effectually neutralized this struggle at the governmental level. He borrowed from the vaunted British model the idea of achieving an equilibrium of the predominant and rival passions and interests within the legislature, albeit without deriving the competing humors from a hereditary ranking.

The key to the success of the British political system was the creation of institutions and practices that neutralize the destabilizing effects of the rival passions in society and at the same time utilize those passions to energize and bolster the government. Hamilton believed that if the American republic was to succeed, it too must incorporate a political scheme that channels men's selfish passions and interests and utilizes them to support the government.[47] Besides force, Hamilton listed four other factors that prompt men to support the government, viz., interest, opinion, habit, and influence.[48] Of these, self-interest is "the most powerful incentive of human action," he argued, explicitly following Hume in his assessment of human nature.[49] No regime derives benefit from neglecting to utilize this dominant force in man, Hamilton declared in 1775. He restated this idea at the Constitutional Convention: the key to constructing a stable and good government is to interest the passions of men and make them serve the public.[50]

---

[45] Ibid.

[46] Harvey Flaumenhaft, *The Effective Republic: Administration and Constitution in the Thought of Alexander Hamilton* (Durham, N.C.: Duke University Press, 1992), 186.

[47] "New York Ratifying Convention. First Speech of June 25 (Francis Child's version)," *PAH* 5:85.

[48] Alexander Hamilton's notes for "Speech on a Plan of Government," June 18, 1787, *PAH* 4:180.

[49] "The Farmer Refuted," *PAH* 1:92.

[50] Alexander Hamilton's notes for "Speech on a Plan of Government," June 18, 1787, *PAH* 4:187; "Remarks on the Ineligibility of Members of the House of Representatives for Other Offices," *PAH* 4:217.

The conjunction between Hamilton's economic and political philosophies occurs at two principal axes. First, Hamilton believed that economic diversification is necessary to the security of individual rights. Second, he held that economic prosperity leads to an opinion of confidence in government, thereby providing the foundation for public strength. The diversification of occupations throughout the union, he predicted, would contribute significantly to overcoming the rivalry between northern and southern interests, that is, between industry and agriculture, between free and slaveholding states.[51] Economic diversification would help to control the problem of majority faction by diminishing the most powerful engine of faction in America – interests grounded in geographic/occupational distinctions. Moreover, increased diversification would lead to a preponderance of members of the learned professions, especially the legal profession, in Congress. Unlike men of industry and agriculture, men of the professional ranks "form no distinct interest in society" and are likely to be impartial arbiters between the others.[52] Economic diversification also fuels prosperity, and vice versa. Economic prosperity instills in the people an opinion of the benefit of government to their own well-being and inspires in them a confidence in its measures. Public confidence in government stabilizes the regime and endows it with public strength. This is particularly true in republican government, which, even more than other political forms, depends on opinion.[53]

[51] "Alexander Hamilton's Final Version of the Report on the Subject of Manufactures," *PAH* 10:293; see also Richard Brookhiser, *Alexander Hamilton: American* (New York: Free Press, 1999), 97. According to Brookhiser, Hamilton believed that the "'Ideas of contrariety of interests' between the North and the South ... are 'as unfounded as they are mischievous'" and that "'the diversity of circumstances' between the regions in fact leads to a 'contrary conclusion,' because 'mutual wants constitute one of the strongest links of political connection.'" Brookhiser summarizes Hamilton's view thus: "If the South wanted to be a region of farms, let the North supply her hats and wires."

[52] *Federalist* 35:183; see also William B. Allen, with Kevin A. Cloonan, *The Federalist: A Commentary* (New York: Peter Lang, 2000), 167–74.

[53] "New York Ratifying Convention: First Speech of June 21 (Francis Child's version)," *PAH* 5:37. For an innovative and thought-provoking defense of Hamilton's ideas and policies regarding commerce, statesmanship, and public opinion, see Michael D. Chan, *Aristotle and Hamilton: On Commerce and Statesmanship* (Columbia: University of Missouri Press, 2006). "Hamilton's America," Chan argues, "was industrious, entrepreneurial, innovative, temperate, sagacious, energetic, diverse, urbane, mobile, refined, and lawful" (183). In contrast to the Jeffersonian and Madisonian vision of an agricultural nation filled with independent yeoman farmers, Hamilton "aimed at nothing less than a change in the American character." Chan agrees with my claim that Hamilton's promotion of the commercial industrialization of America was "less broadly participatory than Madison's," but he further argues that Hamilton would not restrict the role of statesmen to inspiring confidence in the citizens (59, n. 4). Hamilton believed that opinion is the arbiter of governmental measures. Thus, it is not simply statesmen who must be enlightened; "the people, or public opinion,

In 1787 the United States was predominantly an agricultural nation. To achieve Hamilton's goals of economic diversification and prosperity meant that America must become a commercial and industrial republic. This transformation depended on the institution of his three-pronged fiscal program, beginning with the establishment of public credit and a national bank and culminating in governmental support of manufactures. Accordingly, Hamilton sought to connect the interests of the monied men to the interests of the nation – an idea he never dispensed with.[54] The first wave of his economic program depended on this connection. It would stabilize public credit, wean men from state attachments to the support of the national government, and provide the avenue for economic prosperity and the train of events that would usher in a new economic and political era in America. Like Montesquieu, Hamilton believed that in a republic, where all the passions are free and unmodified, it is natural that the passion for material aggrandizement dominates men's souls.[55] A commercial republic allows the passionate pursuit of economic gain and rewards it with success. Commercial prosperity multiplies "the means of gratification," promotes the circulation of charming, shiny metals – "those darling objects of human avarice and enterprise" – and increases prosperity throughout the society.[56] The multiplication of the means of gratifying the acquisitive desire is much more the result of economic prosperity than of the mere size of the territory. By interesting the monied men in the prosperity of the nation, Hamilton sought to start a chain reaction that would promote the commercialization of the entire nation. The consequences of this economic metastasis were far-reaching on the political

must also be enlightened, and not only about matters of fundamental or constitutional opinion; but to the extent possible, enlightenment must extend to matters of policy" (61). I would agree that Hamilton placed great importance on "opinion," and that to the "extent possible" he sought to educate and enlighten opinion in the American republic, as his many public reports and articles demonstrate. Nonetheless, he disagreed with the Republicans about the extent to which public enlightenment is possible and thus was ultimately forced to make his case to the people in the hope of achieving more than he believed the public understanding could bear.

54 Forrest McDonald claims that in his maturity Hamilton rejected the idea of tying the interests of the wealthy to the interest of government, pointing particularly to his seemingly modified argument in 1795 in "The Defence of the Funding System" (*Novus Ordo Seclorum* [Lawrence: University Press of Kansas, 1985], 137). Hamilton's argument in "The Defence," however, is more nuanced. Although Hamilton claims that the bonding of the interests of the monied men to the national interest was not his primary aim in his plan to fund the debt – indeed, that it was the consideration upon which he relied the least – it was nonetheless included in his calculation. See *PAH* 19:40–41; cf. Hamilton to Unknown Recipient, December, 1779–March, 1780, *PAH* 2:248).

55 Montesquieu, *SOL* 19:27, 325,328.

56 *Federalist* 12:59.

front. By multiplying and diversifying occupations and interests in America, the age-old battle between the haves and have-nots would be replaced by a new and much less dangerous rivalry in society. The likelihood of a majority faction forming would be greatly reduced and the stability of the political order would be significantly enhanced. Moreover, the commercial republic possesses the advantage over other forms of government because it tends "to interest the passions of the community in its favor [and] beget[s] public spirit and public confidence."[57]

Hamilton viewed human nature as consisting of two very different types of men: the mass of men who are motivated largely by self-interest and an exclusive class of men whose souls are dominated by the desire for distinction. Hamilton accepted the generality of human nature as it was and did not attempt to transform it into something it could not become. He relied on the average republican citizen to pursue his own economic advantage, neither expecting nor encouraging him to develop a public-spiritedness unconnected with his perception of self-interest. The vast majority of citizens were not called on to participate actively in the affairs of government; the extent of their peacetime responsibilities was essentially limited to electing the better sort of men to political office and supporting the government they had chosen.[58] Their attachment to the new American republic, Hamilton believed, would result largely from their opinion of its necessity and utility.

A train of prosperous events, brought about by a wise and energetic administration, would engender an attachment of the people to their government and instill in them confidence in its measures.[59] "The confidence of the people will be easily gained by a good administration," Hamilton maintained.[60] Confidence results largely from the gratification of men's acquisitive desires, producing habits of obligation and obedience to government. Since all governments, and particularly free republics, are dependent on public opinion, the wise republican statesman will cultivate an opinion of confidence by promoting measures that gratify the average citizen's passion for material gain, thereby increasing the stability and strength of the nation. In turn, the statesman himself is rewarded by the favor of public opinion, that is, by the confidence and esteem of his fellow citizens, thus gratifying

---

[57] "Notes Taken in the Federal Convention," *PAH* 4:163.

[58] "The Continentalist No. VI," *PAH* 3:102–3; "Second Letter from Phocion," April, 1784, *PAH* 3:544–45. Cf. Flaumenhaft, *The Effective Republic*, 15–16, 216.

[59] "New York Ratifying Convention: First Speech of June 21 (Francis Child's version)," *PAH* 5:39–40.

[60] Ibid., *PAH* 5:39.

his distinctive desire for fame. In this way, the most powerful passions of the many and the ruling passion of the noblest minds are directed toward the support of government.[61]

Hamilton learned, perhaps from Jacques Necker, the importance of directing public opinion to the support of government by means of publicity, particularly publicity in the area of national finance. Necker's theory emphasized the influence of public ministers on public opinion to produce unity, confidence, and obedience to the government. "A skilful administration," he wrote, "has the effect of putting in action those it persuades, of strengthening the moral ideas, of rousing the imagination and of joining together the opinions and sentiments of men by the confidence it inspires."[62] Confidence is "that precious sentiment which unites the future to the present" and "lays the surest foundation of the happiness of the people."[63] Hamilton took Necker's advice and wrote prolifically for the public press in an effort to influence public opinion and inspire a spirit of confidence in the government and obedience to its measures. Although Hamilton believed that the citizens generally possess the ability to perceive their interests with sufficient clarity, he also recognized that they are sometimes misled by opinions built on false appearances of the advantageous.[64]

Hamilton believed that disadvantageous policies can also result from affections of the heart. At the start of the second Washington administration and the outbreak of war between France and Great Britain, Hamilton feared that the Republicans' "womanish attachment" to the new French republic and animus against England could result in an American foreign policy that would destroy his entire financial program. Hamilton took measures to prevent this from happening. He was a major force behind Washington's issuance of the 1793 Neutrality Proclamation, he defended the proclamation in a series of "Pacificus" essays, and in 1795–96 he published numerous

[61] In contrast to the widespread desire for economic gain, the love of fame, which Hamilton called the "ruling passion of the noblest minds," is clearly not an objective promoted by the commercial republic (*Federalist* 72:405). Ralph Lerner has remarked, "What, Hamilton asked, was to be done about men whose aspirations fell only sometimes within the ordinary system of rewards held out by a [commercial] republic – men of 'irregular ambition,' intent on seizing or even creating chances for self-promotion? (*Federalist* 72:408) To this challenge the commercial republicans responded with counsel and modest hopes, but no sure solution. The limits of the market model were in sight" ("Commerce and Character: The Anglo-American as New-Model Man," *William and Mary Quarterly* 36:1 [1979], 18).

[62] Jacques Necker, *A Treatise on the Administration of the Finances of France*, 3 vols., Thomas Mortimer, trans. (London: J. Walter, 1785), 1:xii.

[63] Ibid., 1:x.

[64] Stourzh, *Alexander Hamilton and the Idea of Republican Government*, 92–93.

pieces defending the Jay Treaty, which clarified and ensured continued commercial relations with Great Britain. Going head to head with Helvidius (i.e.,
Madison) in the paper wars, he argued for a construction of the Constitution that recognized the conduct of foreign policy as essentially executive in
nature, though he allowed for the constitutional role of the Senate in making
treaties and of the Congress in its power to declare war. He would not agree
with Madison, however, that the constitutional powers granted to Congress
delimit the constitutional and practical duties of the executive to conduct
foreign policy. Once again, in Hamilton's mind, the proper construction of
the Constitution intersected with political and economic realities. Indeed,
he believed that the continuance of stable political relations and a dynamic
commerce with Great Britain were absolutely critical to America's future.[65]
Great Britain provided a major market for American agricultural produce,
and approximately three-fourths of United States imports came from Britain.
American prosperity, and the civic confidence it inspired in government,
depended heavily on the revenues brought into the United States Treasury
from impost duties on British goods. If American dependence on commerce
with England were to lessen with the rise of a diversified domestic economy,
this would occur only over a period of time. Until then, a significant decline
or loss of British trade would ruin the United States economy, destroy public
credit, and shake the political foundations of the fledgling country. The policy of commercial discrimination against the British – which Madison had
been pushing for in Congress since 1789 – would result in British retaliation
against the United States and be devastating to the new nation.[66] In a word,
it could vastly delay, if not destroy, the Hamiltonian dream of commercial
greatness for America.

Out of office and focused on his private legal practice during the Adams
administration, Hamilton only occasionally acted as counselor to the Federalist Party. One of these occasions was in 1798. Due to the perceived threat
posed by some Americans' (i.e., Republicans') attachment to France over
and above loyalty to their own country, the Federalists drafted the Alien
and Sedition Acts. When first shown a draft of the acts, Hamilton approved
the former but protested the latter, arguing that the Sedition Act contained
"highly exceptional" provisions. "I hope sincerely the thing may not be
hurried through," he wrote Treasury Secretary Oliver Wolcott. "Let us not

---

[65] Elkins and McKitrick, *The Age of Federalism*, 123–31; cf. Jack Rakove, *James Madison and the Creation of the American Republic* (Glenview, Ill.: Scott, Foresman/Little, Brown Higher Education, 1990), 118.

[66] Compare Hamilton's position after the formation of the new government with his argument for commercial regulations against the British in *Federalist* 11.

establish a tyranny. Energy is a very different thing from violence."[67] Ultimately, however, Hamilton supported an amended version of the Sedition Act. In general, he believed that truth should be allowed as a defense against the charge of libel; if a defendant could prove that his statements were true, the jury (and not the judge, as in the British common law tradition) should consider this in its verdict.[68] Despite the somewhat liberalizing tendency of American libel laws at the turn of the nineteenth century, the Sedition Act was no more acceptable to the American public than the Alien Act. Indeed, the acts became a major issue in the election of 1800 and contributed to the defeat of the Federalist Party.

During the 1790s, Hamilton's earlier sanguinity about the effects easily gained by a good administration was destroyed by the successes of opponents whom he thought misjudged or misled the common man. He believed that naive projectors and ambitious demagogues had instigated a systematic opposition to his economic measures. Aaron Burr clearly fit the description of the ambitious demagogue.[69] Jefferson had something of the demagogue in him, Hamilton believed, but was fundamentally a man whom nature had ill endowed with a "sublimated paradoxical imagination."[70] Having drunk too much from the well of French philosophy, his "mind [was] prone to projects ... incompatible with the principles of stable and systematic government."[71] Madison, at least initially, appeared to Hamilton a different sort of man. At the commencement of the new government, Hamilton claimed, there existed a similarity of thinking between Madison and himself. Despite their disagreement on debt discrimination and the assumption of state debts, Hamilton remained disposed to believe in Madison's honesty, fairness, and goodwill. After all, not only had they worked in tandem to produce *The Federalist*, they had also spent considerable time at the outset of the new government exchanging ideas and friendly advice. They must have appeared to those around them, and to themselves as well, as political allies. By the

---

[67] Hamilton to Oliver Wolcott, June 29, 1798, *PAH* 21:522. Cf. McDonald, *Alexander Hamilton* (New York: W. W. Norton, 1979), 339 and n. 20; Chernow, *Alexander Hamilton*, 571–72; John C. Miller, *Alexander Hamilton & the Growth of the New Nation* (New York: Transaction Publishers, 2003), 484–85; Martin, "Reforming Republicanism," 109–33.

[68] See Martin, "Reforming Republicanism, 118–28. See also James Morton Smith, "Alexander Hamilton, the Alien Law, and Seditious Libels," *Review of Politics* 16:3 (1954), 305–33; Karl-Friedrich Walling, *Republican Empire: Alexander Hamilton on War and Free Government* (Lawrence: University Press of Kansas, 1999), 249–56, 261–62.

[69] Hamilton to James A. Bayard, January 16, 1801, *PAH* 25:321.

[70] Hamilton to Charles Cotesworth Pinckney, October 10, 1792, *PAH* 12:544.

[71] "Catullus No. IV," *PAH* 12:581; Hamilton to Edward Carrington, May 26, 1792, *PAH* 11:439.

spring of 1792, however, Hamilton became convinced that Madison was acting in cooperation with Jefferson, that he was actuated by "personal and political animosity" against him, and that his character was in fact subtle, complicated, and artificial in a way that the treasury secretary had not previously understood.[72] Either Jefferson had so influenced Madison that the latter had undergone a material change of mind or Madison was simply a common political calculator, pursuing measures to feed his own political popularity and/or the advantage of his particular state.[73] Whatever Madison's motives, by 1792 the Roman alliance between the two leading Publii of 1787–88 was shattered forever.

Although Hamilton initially speculated that Madison's opposition was motivated by personal ambition or partisan rivalry, possibly resulting from Jefferson's influence over him, he later acknowledged what Madison had long claimed – that the war between Republicans and Federalists stemmed from a difference of principle. "[I]n reality the foundations of society, the essential interests of our nation, the dearest concerns of individuals are staked upon the eventful contest," Hamilton wrote in 1801.[74] "[T]he contest between us is indeed a war of principles" – not a war "between monarchy and republicanism" but "between tyranny and liberty."[75] Hamilton's modification of his earlier perspective is often overlooked by scholars, perhaps because it is easy to see it as just another partisan shot at his political opponents. Yet this is precisely what Hamilton warned his contemporaries against: those who persist in seeing the conflict as nothing more than zealous partisanship and a struggle for power are deceived.

Hamilton's more mature and, I would argue, more trenchant assessment of the party contest provides a valuable insight into the democratic implications of Madison's and the Republicans' agenda. It also has a virtue that is lacking in Hamilton's earlier assessment and in much of the scholarly analysis of this era: it allows Madison his own voice rather than merely subsuming it under Hamilton's "Publius" in the 1780s or Jefferson's sway in the 1790s. Ultimately, Hamilton recognized that Madison's opposition to him and the Federalists was propelled by a fundamental philosophic disagreement over the nature and role of public opinion in a republic. Apparently, Jefferson was not alone in his attachment to a "wild and fatal" political

---

[72] Hamilton to Edward Carrington, May 26, 1792, *PAH* 11:432–34.

[73] See, for example, Forrest McDonald's endorsement of this thesis in *Alexander Hamilton*, 199–200, 175, 254, and in *The Presidency of George Washington* (New York: W. W. Norton, 1974), 80–81.

[74] "An Address to the Electors of the State of New York," *PAH* 25:352–53.

[75] Ibid., *PAH* 25:370.

scheme that would destroy sound government in America.[76] Like the French writers from whose well of speculative philosophy they were imbibing, the Republicans were bent on a fanaticism in politics that miscalculated the force of the human passions and was "unsuited to the nature of man."[77] They were simply "too much in earnest" about "democracy."[78] Prostrating themselves before the opinion of the majority, as if *vox populi* were *vox dei*, they encouraged a spirit of anarchy and flirted with tyranny, its natural ally. They stimulated the restless passions of the people and excited a reckless censure, destroying public confidence in the government and its leaders.[79] Following in the path of their Jacobin cohorts, the Republicans worshiped at the altar of the "Goddess of Reason," rejecting the "mild reign of rational liberty, which rests on the basis of an efficient and well balanced government."[80]

Men are for the most part ruled by their passions, Hamilton believed, and are rather more "reasoning tha[n] reasonable animals."[81] Yet his opponents were intent on molding "a wise, reflecting and dispassionate people." They eulogized reason, but in reality they courted men's vanities and cheated the people out of their confidence. Left unchecked, the Republican brand of politics would succeed in "corrupting public opinion till it becomes fit for nothing but mischief."[82] Moreover, they claimed for public opinion a moral status in free government and invoked its authority to circumvent the prescribed constitutional amendment process – the only legitimate channel of appeal to the people in their collective capacity.[83] The Republican politics of public opinion threatened to undermine all the hard work done by the men at Philadelphia in 1787, and the source of their new creed was none other than the fanatics of the French Enlightenment. Hamilton named names:

In vain was the collected wisdom of America convened at Philadelphia. In vain were the anxious labours of a Washington bestowed. Their works are regarded as nothing better than empty bubbles destined to be blown away by the mere breath of a disciple of *Turgot*; a pupil of *Condorcet*.[84]

[76] Hamilton to Washington, August 18, 1792, *PAH* 12:249; "Views on the French Revolution," *PAH* 26:740.
[77] "Views on the French Revolution," *PAH* 26:739.
[78] Hamilton to James A. Bayard, January 16, 1801, *PAH* 25:319.
[79] "Treasury Department Circular to the Commissioners of Loans," *PAH* 13:394–95.
[80] "An Address to the Electors of the State of New York," *PAH* 25:353, 370.
[81] Hamilton to James A. Bayard, April [16–21], 1802, *PAH* 25:605.
[82] Ibid., *PAH* 25:605–6.
[83] Ibid., *PAH* 25:606.
[84] "The Examination. Number IX," *PAH* 25:501.

Whatever diminution of respect Hamilton had felt in the early 1790s for the force of Madison's mind and the soundness of his judgment, a decade later his opinion of the Virginian's political sagacity had sunk lower still. From Hamilton's perspective, the loss of Madison as a political and philosophic ally must have been a genuine disappointment. This was the mind that had conspired with him at the Constitutional Convention, penned with him *The Federalist*, and seemed to understand, if not fully, at least better than most of his colleagues, the age-old dilemma of the few versus the many and the republican road that could overcome it.

3

Madison and the French Enlightenment

Hamilton's fears about the influence of French Enlightenment philosophy on Jefferson and Madison were not ungrounded. Certainly Jefferson's views were significantly shaped by the French authors whom he read and associated with during his ministerial stint in Paris. In the 1780s and 1790s Madison too was a keen scholar of French social and political thought, studying the more radical thought of Turgot, Condorcet, and the physiocrats, as well as the more moderate philosophy of the celebrated oracle, the Baron de Montesquieu.

In the provocative Party Press Essay "Spirit of Governments," Madison first bestowed rather circumscribed praise on Montesquieu's contributions to the science of politics; he then swiftly turned his pen against the classification of governmental types set forth in *The Spirit of Laws*.[1] Montesquieu's typology of governmental forms, Madison asserted, "can never be defended against the criticism which it has encountered." Despite his partial comprehension of the truths of politics, Montesquieu was not in the same league as Newton or Locke, "who established immortal systems" in matter and mind, respectively.[2] Rather, "he was in his particular science what Bacon was in universal science. He lifted the veil from the venerable errors which enslaved opinion, and pointed the way to those luminous truths of which he had but a glimpse himself."[3]

[1] *PJM* 14:233–34.
[2] "Spirit of Governments," *PJM* 14:233.
[3] Compare Madison's identification of Montesquieu with Bacon rather than Newton with the seventeenth-century historian John Millar's similar statement: "I am happy to acknowledge the obligations I feel myself under to this illustrious philosopher [Adam Smith], by having, at an early period of life, had the benefit of hearing his lectures on the History of Civil Society, and of enjoying his unreserved conversation on the same subject. – The great Montesquieu

Montesquieu's influence on Madison and the American Founders, particularly evident in the theory of separation of powers that informs the United States Constitution, is well noted by scholars.⁴ Madison's pointed critique of Montesquieu in the 1790s, however, has been given scant attention.⁵ The crux of Madison's criticism concerned the Frenchman's praise of the British system of balanced government. According to Montesquieu, the institutional and corporate division of powers and checks and balances established in the British system of government provided for political moderation and made the English constitution the model of free government in the modern world.⁶ Most English politicians and writers, whether of the Court or Country party, agreed with the general assumptions underlying the theory of balanced government advocated by Montesquieu; their disagreement was among themselves and essentially concerned whether the parts of their government were effectively separated and balanced, and thus whether liberty was or was not sufficiently protected. Conversely, a number of French thinkers disagreed with Montesquieu's assumptions, rejecting their countryman's theory of balanced government as any real guarantee of stability or safeguard for liberty. When Madison publicly invoked the name of Montesquieu in his writings of the early 1790s, it was primarily to challenge rather than to celebrate the political wisdom of the French oracle. His

---

pointed out the road. He was the Lord Bacon in this branch of philosophy. Dr. Smith is the Newton" (John Millar, *An Historical View of the English Government*, 4 vols., Mark Salber Phillips and Dale R. Smith, eds. [Indianapolis: Liberty Fund, 2006], II:404–5). Adam Smith was Millar's teacher at the University of Glasgow. According to Phillips and Smith, "Millar's footnote to this section is an often-quoted tribute to his teacher, and it expresses the view that, while Montesquieu was the pioneer of the Enlightenment's naturalistic approach to the study of human society, Smith was its true founder." While Madison compares Montesquieu to Bacon, he does not mention Adam Smith as analogous to Newton or mention Smith at all.

⁴ In a seminal study of philosophic referents by the Founding generation, Donald Lutz has shown that Montesquieu ranks significantly above all else, including John Locke ("The Relative Influence of European Writers on Late Eighteenth-Century American Political Thought," *American Political Science Review* 78:1 [1984], 189–97). Yet, as Lutz points out, heavier referencing does not necessarily imply greater agreement; a proportion of the citations to a particular political philosopher may demonstrate disagreement with that thinker.

⁵ John Zvesper (*Political Philosophy and Rhetoric: A Study of the Origins of American Political Parties* [Cambridge: Cambridge University Press, 1977], 114–15), Paul A. Rahe (*Republics Ancient and Modern: Classical Republicanism and the American Revolution* 3 vols. [Chapel Hill: University of North Carolina Press, 1994], 3:180–81), and Lance Banning (*The Jeffersonian Persuasion* [Ithaca, N.Y.: Cornell University Press, 1978], 167–68; *The Sacred Fire of Liberty: James Madison & the Founding of the Federal Republic* [Ithaca, N.Y.: Cornell University Press, 1995], 358–59) briefly discuss Madison's alternative categorization of governmental types and identify the type that operates "by corrupt influence" as an unmistakable reference to the British government, as well as to U.S. administration policies of the 1790s.

⁶ Montesquieu, *SOL* 11:6, 156–66.

criticisms, like those of many Continental writers, signaled a fundamental disagreement with Montesquieu's analysis of free government.

Madison's proposed alternative to Montesquieu's vaunted British model is grounded in the recognition of public opinion as the ruling authority in republican government. The concept of public opinion as a dominant political force originated in France in the late 1760s and was popularized by Jacques Necker in *De l'administration des finances de la France*, published in 1784. In the years leading up to the French Revolution, a host of French writers touted the reign of public opinion and the advent of a new kind of politics. Madison was familiar with much of this material in the 1780s and continued his study of French texts in the 1790s, demonstrating a keen interest in their treatment of *l'opinion publique*. The almost singular reliance by scholars on British thinkers as sources of influence on Madison's political thought, and the virtual neglect of French theorists, surely calls for reconsideration. Interestingly, the spur to French thinking on this subject was the great sage Montesquieu, who pioneered the path to the politics of public opinion, even though he himself did not complete the journey.

Montesquieu's categorization of regime types consists of despotism, monarchy, and republicanism, including aristocratic and democratic republicanism. Each type is characterized by a predominant spirit: the first by fear, the second by honor, and the third by virtue.[7] Montesquieu's observations concerning the British government are tantamount to the introduction of a fourth governmental species, or at least to a new definition of republican government. In response to Montesquieu, Madison suggested an alternative categorization of regime types. The first kind of government he described consists of a permanently armed military force that compels the submission of the populace. The second governmental type is activated by private interest and corrupt influence, and the third governmental form operates on the basis of the reason of the society.

Madison depicted the first kind of government as inhumane, operating on a burdened and plagued people who groan under its oppressive weight. Examples of this kind of government are numerous throughout history, and in the present time, Madison observed, still operate in "almost every country of Europe." While they pride themselves on their marks of civilization and humanity, they are not substantially different from the despotic governments that have dominated the globe throughout the ages. This description would certainly include China, Turkey, Spain, and the ancien régime of France. The British government is described in Madison's second category, which

7 Ibid., *SOL* 2:1–2, 10; 3:1–9, 21–29.

bolsters partisan corruption with the threat of military force. However, as Madison noted in the introduction to his analysis, governments are seldom if ever reducible to a single principle of operation. Nonetheless, whenever possible, it is useful to identify the spirit that predominates in them.

Madison's second governmental type functions by unleashing the motive of private interest, utilizing avidity as a substitute for public duty. By distributing bounties to allies and bribes to opponents, it is supported by "an army of interested partizans." The wagging tongues, the pens, the intrigues, and the political alignments of these corrupt backers supply "the terror of the sword." While it may pretend to represent the liberty of the many, in actuality it is dominated by the few. "Such a government," Madison declared,

wherever to be found, is an imposter. It is happy for the new world that it is not on the west side of the Atlantic. It will be both happy and honorable for the United States, if they never descend to mimic the costly pageantry of its forms, nor betray themselves into the venal spirit of its administration.

The vaunted liberty of this governmental type is largely a pretext, which is discoverable if one examines the spirit and principle of its operations. There can be no doubt that the government Madison is describing here is that of England and that he identified the predominant spring of its operations as pecuniary self-interest. Certainly his contemporaries recognized in this derisive appraisal certain aspects of the British government that were admired by many. In *The Spirit of Laws* Montesquieu deliberately evaded identifying the operating principle and spirit of the British government, choosing instead to emphasize that liberty constitutes its direct end.[8] Madison's criticism of Montesquieu's analysis in "Spirit of Governments" is due to this evasion, which provided the grounds for categorizing Great Britain as a type of free government or republic. The vigor of Madison's censure was intensified by the acceptance of this categorization by influential citizens of his own country, especially John Adams and Alexander Hamilton. Thus, his explicit invocation of Montesquieu's errors in this article was motivated by both philosophic and practical political concerns.

In "British Government,"[9] an article published in the *National Gazette* just three weeks prior to "Spirit of Governments," Madison took a different tack in criticizing Montesquieu. In this essay he implicitly invoked Montesquieu's analysis of the British constitution to demonstrate that it is rooted in historical error. The equilibrium of the British government (such

[8] Ibid., *SOL* 11:5, 156; 11:20, 186.
[9] "British Government," *PJM* 14:201–2.

as it is), Madison argued, is not primarily ascribable to its particular form of distributed powers. Those who attribute the longevity of the British constitution to this cause forget the changes that have occurred over time. In primitive times, the executive and the judicial power were combined and the legislature consisted of a single chamber; at present, the government is divided into three branches with a bicameral legislature. If the current government is characterized by a balance of power, the older form lacked any balance at all, yet it lasted longer than the current one has even been tried. The primary cause of the preservation of governmental equilibrium, Madison claimed, is "the force of public opinion." Absent this force, the power balance of the current government would likely shift to either the monarch or the House of Commons. Either the "ambition in the House of Commons could wrest from [the monarch] his prerogatives, or the avarice of its members, might sell to him its privileges."

Madison implicitly took issue with the theory of corporate governmental equilibrium in his *National Gazette* essay "Parties."[10] Published a few days before "British Government" appeared, it presented a brief description of the balanced government theory that Madison would attribute directly to the British system in the later article. Although different interests and parties arise naturally in all political societies, Madison asserted, the notion that the encouragement of a conflict of interests in society is beneficial to the equilibrium of the political order is nonsense. The idea that the different social and corporate classes should each possess a certain portion of governmental power in order to balance each other is consistent neither with reason nor with republican theory. The encouragement of partial and/or artificial interests to promote political conflict and achieve political equilibrium is not the secret of Britain's (apparent) liberty, stability, and success. Madison's critique of the English system points to a fundamental disagreement with Montesquieu, Hume, and others over the essential character of republican government. Building on their nascent insight into the relationship of public opinion to the stability of political order, Madison argued that not only is public opinion the actual ground of political power and stability in every government, it is the only genuine sovereign authority in free government.[11]

In the third category of regime types in "Spirit of Governments" Madison showcased republican government and contrasted it with the preceding two

---

[10] "Parties," *PJM* 14:197–98.

[11] "Public Opinion," *PJM* 14:170. In Madison's "Notes on Government" (*PJM* 14:157–69), a portion of which served as draft notes for some of the Party Press Essays, Madison entitled one of the sections "Influence of Public Opinion on Government." Madison obviously drew from this segment of the "Notes" when writing both "British Government" and "Public Opinion" for the *National Gazette*.

types of regimes. Anchored in public opinion, this government derives "its energy from the will of the society, and operat[es] by the reason of its measures, on the understanding and interest of the society."[12] Madison continued in an uncharacteristically rhapsodic timbre:

[This] is the government for which philosophy has been searching, and humanity been sighing, from the most remote ages. Such are the republican governments which it is the glory of America to have invented, and her unrivalled happiness to possess.

Montesquieu "glimpsed" the elegance of the theory underlying a republic of this character, but like Locke, he suffered from the disadvantage "of having written before these subjects were illuminated by the events and discussions which distinguish a very recent period."[13] In addition, Montesquieu was unfortunately "warped by a regard to the particular government of England, . . . profess[ing] admiration bordering on idolatry."[14]

Madison's writings in the early 1790s reveal that his theory of republican government cannot be understood simply or even primarily within the context of the philosophy of Montesquieu – or Hume or Locke – or any of the British thinkers who relied on Montesquieu's analysis. Indeed, his theory can be accurately grasped only if the distinctions he marked out between Montesquieu and himself are fully taken into account. In Madison's view, the lucid picture of the principles and processes of republican government accessible to him and his generation was clouded in the decades in which Locke and Montesquieu lived and wrote. According to Keith Michael Baker, the concept of public opinion as a political force did not generally emerge until about 1770.[15] Its emergence in France under the ancien régime, however, changed the face of French political thought and politics throughout the remainder of the century and beyond.

---

[12] "Spirit of Governments," *PJM* 14:234.

[13] Madison, "Helvedius No. I," *PJM* 15:68.

[14] Ibid.

[15] Keith Michael Baker, *Inventing the French Revolution: Essays on French Political Culture in the Eighteenth Century* (Cambridge: Cambridge University Press, 1990), 187. The numerous works by Baker on the society and politics of eighteenth-century France, and particularly his writings on the concept of public opinion during this era, are a pathbreaking and brilliant contribution to understanding the political thought of French thinkers during this period. Also excellent is Mona Ozouf's work, particularly "'Public Opinion' at the End of the Old Regime," Lydia C. Cochrane, trans., *The Journal of Modern History* 60 Supplement (1988), S1–S21. See also Harvey Chisick, "Public Opinion and Political Culture in France During the Second Half of the Eighteenth Century," *English Historical Review* 117 (2002), 48–77. For a comprehensive treatment of the concept of public opinion in French thought see J. A. W. Gunn, *Queen of the World: Opinion in the Public Life of France from the Renaissance to the Revolution* (Oxford: Voltaire Foundation, 1995).

During Jefferson's stint as ambassador to the court of Louis XVI, he routinely purchased and sent books to his friend in Virginia. Some of the volumes shipped were ones specifically requested by Madison, while others were selected by Jefferson for him, sometimes with a line or two in his letters relaying his own enthusiasm for a selected author or work. Among the books and pamphlets Jefferson sent Madison during the late 1780s were works by Mably, Moreau, Necker, Turgot, Condorcet, Chastellux, DuPont de Nemours, Le Trosne, Louis-Sébastien Mercier, Le Mercier de La Rivière, Volney, comte de Mirabeau, Brissot de Warville, Barthélemy, and Panckoucke's edition of the *Encyclopédie méthodique* as these volumes became available.[16] Madison also obtained earlier from France writings by La Bruyère and Raynal's work on the East and West Indies. With the exception of texts by Condorcet and Raynal, Madison included works by these French authors in his list of books bound for Philadelphia in 1790.[17] Surely he had a purpose in mind when he selected these texts for shipment to his new residence in the capital city. In the spring of 1791 he penned the "Notes on Government," and later that year and into the next he composed the Party Press Essays. Both the "Notes on Government" and the Party Press Essays incorporate ideas from these French texts. What the French authors just cited (or in the case of Necker, a Swiss employed by the French government) have in common is a conception of a public possessing a judgment and force that cannot safely be ignored by government. In general, they argued that public opinion reflects a moral consensus and is a source of political authority and stability in government.

---

[16] Jefferson to Madison, August 2, 1787, *PJM* 10:128–29; Jefferson to Madison, July 31, 1788, *PJM* 11:212, 214 n. 13; Madison to Jefferson, October 17, 1788, *PJM* 11:295; Jefferson to Madison, January 12, 1789, *PJM* 11:413, 414 n. 4 and n. 5; Madison to Jefferson, May 9, 1789, *PJM* 12:142; "Memorandum of Books," ca. August 1790, *PJM* 13:286–89. In Madison's book list of August 1790, indicating the texts he would send to his residence in Philadelphia, he marked those books purchased for him by Jefferson in France ("Memorandum of Books," ca. August 1790, *PJM* 13:286–89). This list is particularly illuminating in respect to Madison's intended plan of study of French texts in the period following the summer of 1790. Some of the authors listed previously are referenced in this book list by text only, as for example the entry "Tableau de Paris" (authored by Louis-Sébastien Mercier) or "Société Politique" (referring to Le Mercier de La Rivière's *L'Ordre naturel et essentiel des sociétés politiques*). Le Trosne's name is misspelled by Madison as "le Trone," though his work, *De l'administration provinciale et de la réforme de l'impôt*, is clearly indicated by Madison's reference to "Admtron. De l'impôt par le Trone." In addition to citing "Neckar on Religion," Madison lists "Examen sur les finances," which likely refers to Necker's *De l'administration des finances de la France*, published in 1784.

[17] See "Memorandum of Books," ca. August 1790, *PJM* 13:286–89. Of the books Madison specially selected to bring with him to Philadelphia, texts by these French authors make up a significant proportion of the overall shipment.

Most scholars agree that Rousseau was the first prominent writer to employ the phrase *l'opinion publique*.[18] By the latter eighteenth century, however, the phrase had taken on a rationalistic aspect distinctly different from Rousseau's conception. For Rousseau, public opinion was comprised of the untutored views of the populace, which result from customs, mores, and habits. At times, Rousseau speaks of public opinion positively and celebrates it as the guardian of public morality, perhaps even, in its consolidated form, as tantamount to the general will. In contrast to other types of law, public opinion "forms the real constitution of the state."[19] At other times, Rousseau speaks of public opinion as prejudice and fashionable whim, viewing it as an obstacle to the achievement of the general will rather than a vehicle for expressing that will. In this sense, public opinion is much too prone to error and to manipulation by the intellectuals and the royal court; as such, it reflects a servile dependence on the opinions of others, manifesting itself as a debasement of taste and character. Either way, Rousseau did not believe that public opinion is refined or enhanced by representative government or the decision-making process of an interactive, deliberative assembly.[20] Unlike later French thinkers on the subject, Jürgen Habermas argues, Rousseau's concept is really one of an "unpublic opinion," which comprises the idea of a "democracy without public debate."[21]

A second group of French thinkers envisioned a type of politics that would publicize governmental measures and encourage public discussion. This new environment of political openness would invite public expression at the same time that it would shape the public views. The concept of public opinion thus took on a more politically dynamic meaning, conveying the notion of a deliberate and authoritative voice within society that results from communicative activity. This group includes the previously cited French authors. It also includes Jacques Peuchet, who authored the section on "*Police et*

---

[18] See, for example, Paul A. Palmer, "The Concept of Public Opinion in Political Theory," in Carl Wittke, ed., *Essays in History and Political Theory, in Honor of C. H. McIlwain* (Cambridge, Mass.: Harvard University Press, 1936), 236. J. A. W. Gunn, however, argues that the term "public opinion" is employed much earlier than 1750 and, though Rousseau may have been the earliest prominent author to use it, he cannot be credited with originating the expression (*Queen of the World*, 122).

[19] See, for example, Jean-Jacques Rousseau, *The Social Contract* II:12, in Lester G. Crocker, ed., *The Social Contract and Discourse on the Origin of Inequality* (New York: Washington Square Press, 1967), 58. Cf. chapter 7, "Launching the Term 'Public Opinion': Jean-Jacques Rousseau," in Elisabeth Noelle-Neumann, *The Spiral of Silence: Our Social Skin* (Chicago: University of Chicago Press, 1993).

[20] Rousseau, *The Social Contract* II:1, 27–28, and III:15, 98–101.

[21] Jürgen Habermas, *The Structural Transformation of the Public Sphere*, Thomas Burger, trans. (Cambridge, Mass: MIT Press, 1989), 98.

municipalités" in the *Encyclopédie méthodique*, which Madison brought with him to Philadelphia. These authors regarded public opinion as "Queen of the world." In the 1780s, the concept of public opinion became so firmly established in the French lexicon that it replaced "opinion" in the new French encyclopedia.[22] Louis-Sébastien Mercier, in the *Tableau de Paris* in 1782, declared that public opinion had become the universal cry and a preponderant, irresistible force in Europe, and that it had caused a great revolution in men's ideas.[23] "In a nation that thinks and talks," the abbé Raynal argued, "public opinion is the rule of government."[24] "It is public opinion which governs," Le Trosne wrote; "it is therefore important to submit to this master."[25] Jacques Necker, the French minister of finance, called public opinion the "spirit of society," a kind of "invisible power" that, though "destitute of treasures, of guards, and armies, dictates its laws in the capital, in the court, and even in the king's palace."[26] "Everything," Necker asserted, "is, more or less, finally influenced by the impulse of the public."[27]

Given the force of public opinion, this group of French thinkers set for themselves the challenge of articulating a kind of political order that would acknowledge the authority of the newly emerged public. At the same time, however, most (Mably, in particular, excepted) followed Rousseau in rejecting the politics of party contestation, which they viewed as destructive to stability and liberty in political life.[28] The tranquil spirit of public opinion,

[22] The 1765 edition of the *Encyclopédie* contains an entry for "Opinion" that makes the traditional distinction between knowledge and opinion, describing the latter as characterized by uncertainty and variability. In the *Encyclopédie méthodique* there is no entry at all for "*opinion*" in the philosophical sections; rather, the term is replaced by "*opinion publique*," which is treated in the political sections on *finances* and *police*, published in the 1780s, and is associated with rationality.

[23] Louis-Sébastien Mercier, *Tableau de Paris: Nouvelle édition*, 12 vols. (Amsterdam, 1782–88), 4:289.

[24] Guillaume Thomas François Raynal, *Histoire philosophique et politique des établissemens... dans les deux Indes* (Amsterdam, 1770), 6:391–92.

[25] Guillaume François Le Trosne, *De l'administration provinciale et de la réforme de l'impôt* (Basel: P. J. Duplain, 1779), 117.

[26] Jacques Necker, *A Treatise on the Administration of the Finances of France*, 3 vols., Thomas Mortimer, trans. (London: J. Walter, 1785), I:lv, I:lviii.

[27] Ibid., 3:461.

[28] On the politics of party contestation, see Baker, *Inventing the French Revolution*, 186. Mably, and Moreau at least early in his career, set themselves apart from most other French theorists of public opinion in arguing that partisan struggles are beneficial to good government since they provide a kind of energy in politics. Later in his life, however, Moreau dispensed with any discussion praising the British system of party politics. Necker, on the other hand, wanted to discourage factionalism and promote unity and tranquility in political life, though he was in general an admirer of the British government, especially its public disclosure of the nation's finances.

they argued, is incompatible with the kind of factionalism that divides men into opposing groups filled with animosity for each other. A united people is beneficial to political order, for in the public concurrence of opinion government derives stability. In contrast, a perpetual state of warring parties, as in the British model of opposition politics, leaves the citizens in a constant state of insecurity and the government, at best, in precarious equilibrium. The vaunted reign of public opinion meant the rejection of the notion that a government organized on the basis of particular classes or orders of society was sufficient to achieve stability in political affairs or provide the basis for a genuine community of citizens. Apparently, Montesquieu's praise of the British government and the spirit of party rankled more than one generation of Frenchmen.

Despite their disagreements with Montesquieu, this second group of French thinkers on public opinion owes its initial insights to him. From his works, particularly *The Spirit of Laws*, they adopted the idea of a general spirit or mind that animates the society and its laws.[29] With Montesquieu they rejected the Hobbesian legalistic solution to political conflict, seeking instead a more penetrating understanding of the complexity of human affairs. Montesquieu's emphasis on communication and the interactive relationship between *moeurs* and laws resonated in their writings. Jean Jacques Barthélemy, in *Voyage of Anacharsis the Younger in Greece*, for example, argued that *moeurs* "restrain the citizen by the fear of public opinion, while the laws only terrify him by the dread of punishment."[30] In the *Encyclopédie méthodique*, Peuchet contended that Montesquieu's inquiry into the relationship of laws and mores was thoroughly enlightened. "[T]he great art of this philosopher," Peuchet wrote, "is that, even when he is mistaken, he compels the reader to think, and shows him the road that leads to truth."[31] In 1797 Simone-Jérôme Bourlet de Vauxcelles summarized the influence of Montesquieu on thinkers of his century. It was particularly to Montesquieu, he said, that one must turn to understand the roots of public opinion and its formation. That was why Montesquieu titled his great book *Esprit*, thus invoking an intellectual principle that animates all else.[32] Indeed, the ringing

---

[29] Montesquieu, *SOL* 19:308–33.

[30] Jean Jacques Barthlélemy, *Travels of Anacharsis the Younger in Greece during the middle of the fourth century before the Christian aera*, 4th ed., 8 vols. (London, 1806), 5:278. Hereafter cited as *Voyage*.

[31] Peuchet, "Discours préliminaire," in *Encyclopédie méthodique: Jurisprudence*, vol. 9, *Police et municipalités*, i–clx (Paris, 1789), clvii.

[32] Gunn, *Queen of the World*, 375. Cf. Alexis de Tocqueville's discussion of *moeurs* in *Democracy in America*, J. P. Mayer, ed. (New York: Harper Perennial, 1969), 287. Tocqueville

cry by the proponents of a politics of public opinion to establish over society an "empire of reason" would seem to have originated in Montesquieu's idea that "*La raison a un empire naturel.*"[33]

Notwithstanding their indebtedness to Montesquieu, these theorists consciously took his insights further, or perhaps in a different direction, than Montesquieu himself was willing to go. Most found fault with his encouragement of party conflict and checks and balances; the physiocrats and Condorcet, in particular, were unsatisfied with the impure reason that dominated his scheme. As Montesquieu himself readily admitted, the model of balanced government he so praised derives its energy from the agitated play of the passions and thus is rather closed to the guidance of reason.[34] The second group of French thinkers on public opinion generally viewed such a system as the antithesis of good government because, they argued, reason, rather than passion or mere will, is the standard for legitimate public decisions. According to their conception, public opinion is not constituted by a mere aggregate of the sentiments of the populace; it is not synonymous with "popular opinion(s)."[35] Thus, their view must be differentiated from Rousseau's perspective. It must also be distinguished from the contemporary view, which conceives of public opinion as discoverable in daily polling aggregates. This distinction is critically important for those of us today who seek to understand the eighteenth-century concept of public opinion. Theirs was not primarily a theory of political popularism; public opinion was not a spontaneous outpouring by the people or an ephemeral tide of popular sentiments and uneducated views.

---

defines *moeurs* in its original Latin meaning, applying it "not only to '*moeurs*' in the strict sense, which might be called habits of the heart, but also to the different notions possessed by men, the various opinions current among them, and the sum of ideas that shape mental habits."

[33] Montesquieu, *De l'esprit des lois* (1748), sixième partie, 28:38, 79. http://classiques.uqac.ca/classiques/montesquieu/de_esprit_des_lois/partie_6/esprit_des_lois_Livre_6.pdf; cf. Montesquieu, *SOL* 28:38, 591.

[34] This phenomenon is associated with England's extreme political liberty. It may, in fact, be one of the reasons Montesquieu does not unqualifiedly endorse the English model. See Paul A. Rahe, "Forms of Government: Structure, Principle, Object, and Aim," in *Montesquieu's Science of Politics: Essays on The Spirit of Laws* (Lanham, Md.: Rowman & Littlefield, 2001), 69–108 and particularly 82–83.

[35] See, for example, Ozouf, "Public Opinion," S8–9, n. 24; Jacques Peuchet, "Discours préliminaire," in *Encyclopédie méthodique: Jurisprudence*, vol. 9, *Police et municipalités* (Paris, 1789), ix–x. Peuchet published a second volume on *police* in 1791. Carol Allen and William B. Allen are currently completing the first English translation of Peuchet's preliminary discourse to his work on *police* in the *Encyclopédie méthodique*. I am grateful to them for sharing their preliminary draft with me.

Condorcet set forth the distinction between *public* opinion and *popular* opinion bluntly. Whereas public opinion is enlightened by the men of letters, popular opinion is that "of the most stupid and misery-stricken part of the people."[36] Necker put it more diplomatically, distinguishing public opinion from the fleeting popular sentiments and views of the populace. In *De l'administration des finances de la France*, which was reprinted in the section on finances in the *Encyclopédie méthodique*, Necker argued:

We must be very careful not to confound that public opinion, which I have delineated, with those rumours of a day, which commonly take their rise in particular societies only, and under certain circumstances. It is not to such a decision that a man capable of being at the head of an extensive administration ought to give way. On the contrary, he ought to know how to despise it; that he may remain firmly attached to that public opinion, which is respectable under all its forms, and which alone is rendered sacred, by reason, time, and a universal conformity of sentiments.[37]

The proponents of a politics of public opinion agreed on the vital importance of the enlightened members of society to the formation of a public voice grounded in reason. For some, the head of state and/or his high-ranking ministers formed the coterie of enlightened men; for others, the literati were tasked with taking the lead in shaping the public mind. For all of them, publicity and communication were critically important to the dissemination of information to the people and the achievement of an enlightened public opinion.

Moreau and Necker emphasized the influence of the king and his ministers on public opinion to produce unity, confidence, and obedience to the government. According to Moreau, a vigorous defender of the monarchy under the ancien régime, public opinion informs the will of the king, but the king, simultaneously, shapes the conscience and opinion of his subjects. In the final analysis, the subjects owe the sovereign and his government their confidence and obedience. Necker argued that "a skilful administration has the effect of putting in action those it persuades, of strengthening the moral ideas, of rousing the imagination and of joining together the opinions and sentiments of men by the confidence it inspires."[38] Indeed, "confidence" is "that precious sentiment which unites the future to the present" and "lays

---

[36] Ozouf, "Public Opinion," S8–9, n. 24.
[37] Necker, *A Treatise*, I:lxv–lxvi. Cf. Léonard Burnard, *Necker et l'Opinion Publique* (Paris: Honoré Champion, Éditeur, 2004).
[38] Necker, *A Treatise*, I:xii.

the surest foundation of the happiness of the people."[39] "The good opinion of the public," Necker passionately declared, is the "dear object of my ambition!"[40] But the idea of wanting "the good opinion of the people," he admitted, was perhaps rather more of wanting "to render it subservient to great undertakings."[41] Necker and Moreau thus argued for a quasi-dynamic theory of public opinion, emphasizing the influence and inspiration of the monarch and his ministry on the sentiments and attachments of the general public. They neglected, however, to inquire into the composition of the public, their priorities, or the possibility of the citizens' enlightenment, thereby leaving the concept of public opinion abstract and amorphous.[42]

A host of French writers moved substantially beyond Moreau and Necker's conception of public opinion as primarily the judgment of the public on the reputation of men of rank or talent and envisioned a more energetic and substantive role for the public in the political life of a nation. Placing a dual emphasis on the influence of the enlightened men on public opinion *and* the directive influence of public opinion on government, they conceived of public opinion as both acted upon and itself an active agent. Physiocrats such as Le Trosne and Mercier de La Rivière sought to enlighten and direct public opinion and create a unified and active citizenry. To accomplish this they advanced the freedom of the press, free public discussion, the influence of laws and/or *moeurs* on public opinion, the reciprocal influence of public opinion on laws, mores and manners, and, most importantly, the subjection of opinion to *évidence*. According to François Quesnay, the founder of the physiocrats and the author of the entry on "*évidence*" in the *Encyclopédie*, the term "signifies a certitude so clear and manifest by itself that the mind cannot deny it."[43] In order to subject public opinion to the commands of *évidence*, a number of physiocrats advocated the establishment of provincial assemblies, conceiving of them as forums by which to form, direct, and unify the opinion of the public.

Eighteenth-century French advocacy of provincial assemblies generally followed Turgot's plan of provincial and national assemblies, definitively presented in *Mémoire sur les municipalités* (actually drafted by Dupont de

---

[39] Ibid., I:x.

[40] Ibid., I:xvii.

[41] Ibid., I:liv–lv.

[42] See Gunn, *Queen of the World*, 293, 325.

[43] François Quesnay, "*Évidence*," in Denis Diderot, Jean Le Rand d'Alembert, et al., eds., *Encyclopédie*, vol. 6 (Paris: Briasson, 1756). Cf. Pierre Rosanvallon, "Political Rationalism and Democracy in France in the 18th and 19th Centuries," *Philosophy & Social Criticism* 28:6 (2002), 687–701.

Nemours on behalf of Turgot in 1775). Turgot argued that the proper formation of public opinion requires the institution of multiple tiers of government that can strain and purify the passions and interests in society. Accordingly, he and others promoted the establishment of a multilayered system of deliberative assemblies that were intended to transform individual wills and preferences into an authoritative consensus grounded in reason. At the primary local level, the right to participate was limited to those with a sufficient amount of landed property, whose rational interests were ensured by their stake in society. At the national level, members of the assembly were to be elected by the owners of property. Presumably, those elected to political office would be the most educated, respected, and capable members of society, thereby coinciding with or taking their cue from the enlightened elite. Their responsibility was not to represent the will or the partial interests of their constituents, but rather the rational interest of the society. In this process, however, Turgot did not mean to alienate the citizens from the public judgments, for the legislative task he envisioned was simultaneously interventionist, educative, and conciliatory. Nonetheless, the encouragement of civic participation in local affairs was an instrumental means and not a political end for Turgot; primarily, he sought to establish a system that encouraged social and political unity and promoted a scheme of rational administration.[44]

The political system Turgot, his student Condorcet, and their friends in the physiocratic camp envisioned held out the promise of the achievement of a public good determined by the harmonious expression of the mutual benefit of the citizens and common interest of the nation. Distinguishing between the unjust rule of mere will and the just rule of reason in society, they sought the establishment of a political process that subjects individual views and narrow interests to *évidence*, transforming them into a unitary public opinion grounded in reason. The public opinion that results from this process should not be confused with popular opinion, they argued. Rather, public opinion is preceded by the opinion of enlightened men and dictated by it; it is the established "body of beliefs held in common by such [average] men" whose "authority sweeps along the opinion of the people."[45] In this way, the will of the society is made to depend on the reason of the society. Accordingly, public opinion constitutes the expression of the rightful authority of a nation. Over time, public opinion and law provide mutual support for each other, deriving their force not merely from habit but from

---

[44] See Ozouf, "Public Opinion," S20.
[45] *CSW*, 221; See also Ozouf, "Public Opinion," S8–9, n. 24.

the effect of "fixed principles and real, proven truths," thereby establishing over society an "empire of reason."[46]

To establish the rule of reason over society, Condorcet attempted to work out a complex scheme of decision making based on mathematical probabilities. The modern scientific method and the aim of objectivity that inspired Condorcet are generally identified as the basis of the rationalism of the Enlightenment.[47] There is another strand of French Enlightenment thought, however, that vigorously opposed this approach to politics and ethics. Jean Jacques Barthélemy and Jacques Peuchet stand out particularly in this regard. They rejected the mathematical treatment of politics and morality and promoted instead the guidance of prudential reason in political life. With his fellow members of the Académie des Inscriptions et Belles-Lettres, Barthélemy fought against the rationalist philosophy of his day, which he believed threatened to eclipse the humanities and the classics.[48] Peuchet also harshly criticized those who reduced reason to mathematical abstractions and neglected human nature.[49] The end of society, Peuchet asserted, is not metaphysical perfection.[50] Enlightenment will not make men perfectly virtuous. Human beings are a composite of reason and passion, and neither can be eliminated from our nature. Although humanity is not susceptible to perfectibility, he argued, we can nonetheless learn from philosophy and

---

[46] *CSW*, 58.

[47] See, for example, Gertrude Himmelfarb, *The Roads to Modernity: The British, French, and American Enlightenments* (New York: Alfred A. Knopf, 1994).

[48] Louis Bertrand, *La Fin du Classicisme et le Retour a l'Antique* (New York: Burt Franklin, 1897), 43–44.

[49] Peuchet may have learned the spirit of moderation in moral and political inquiry from Montesquieu. He certainly believed that some men of his time did not read Montesquieu carefully, and he was particularly critical of his contemporaries who, devoid of a profound understanding, "invoke abstract principles" and neglect an understanding of "the nature of man, about which *L'Esprit des loix* offers great models so instructively" (Peuchet, "Discours préliminaire," clix). Bernard Manin claims that, in the final analysis, Montesquieu's moderation is "rather like Aristotle's prudence: a virtue that makes it possible to work toward universal goals in a world characterized by relative indeterminacy. But for Montesquieu relative indeterminacy does not rest on the same foundation as for Aristotle: it derives not from the contingency of the material world but from the liberty of man. The consequences for action are the same for both authors, however: ordered, rational action toward universal ends is possible in an indeterminate world, because the indeterminacy of the world is only relative. The French revolutionaries, of whom Condorcet may here be taken as a representative type, rejected this prudential rationality couched in the modern form of a theory of moderation. In this opposition the Revolution marks not the triumph of reason over relativism but the victory of one form of rationality over another" ("Montesquieu," in François Furet and Mona Ozouf, eds., *A Critical Dictionary of the French Revolution* [Cambridge, Mass.: Harvard University Press, 1989], 730).

[50] Peuchet, "Discours préliminaire," lv.

from experience how to diminish the evil and make the good more palpable.[51] Accordingly, Peuchet argued for a politics of moderation, calling for the establishment of "the limits of moderation and the rules of a healthy logic" in ethical and political inquiry.[52]

"Public opinion," Peuchet wrote, "has its source in the opinion of enlightened men, whence it gains partisans and becomes the general conviction."[53] The rise of the print media is a necessary condition for the formation of public opinion, for these sources of information and means of communication, combined with the growth of literacy, make possible the enlightenment of the public. Relying explicitly on William Robertson's *History of the Reign of Charles V*, Peuchet situated his treatment of the phenomenon of public opinion within a general historical account of the progress and transformation of European society.[54] Unlike Barthélemy (whose ideas we will explore in Chapter 7), Peuchet claimed that the idea of public opinion was unknown to the ancient world.[55] In modern times, he said, the art of printing has replaced the spoken word as the primary means of political communication, and the publicity that it engenders is possible over an expansive nation and is not limited to the small polities of classical times.[56]

---

[51] Ibid., liv.

[52] Ibid., liii. Cf. xli.

[53] Ibid., x.

[54] Madison cited the Robertson text in his 1791 "Notes on Government." See *PJM* 14:159. In this work Robertson recognized public opinion as a force for political change in civilized nations. See Karen O'Brien, "Robertson's Place in the Development of Eighteenth Century Narrative History," in Stewart J. Brown, ed., *William Robertson and the Expansion of Empire* (Cambridge: Cambridge University Press, 1997), 74–91. O'Brien argues that although Robertson certainly did not assign to the idea of opinion the authoritative role it has in contemporary political life, he nonetheless envisioned a much more demanding and creative role for it than one can find in Hume's rather "passive and normative processes of opinion" (83).

[55] Interestingly, Madison's study of classical political philosophy led him to a different view. In the "Notes on Government" he claims that Aristotle understood that public opinion could influence the government and contribute to its preservation or destruction, citing particularly Aristotle's discussion of the rotation of regimes in Book V, Chapter 12 of the *Politics* ("Notes on Government," *PJM* 14:162). It is very possible that Madison's commentary on Aristotle's conception of public opinion was a response to Peuchet's and/or others' claims that the ancients were unaware of the idea or force of public opinion. Barthélemy's suggestions regarding Aristotle's understanding of the relationship of *moeurs* and public opinion, and their effect on the preservation or destruction of regimes, may have contributed to Madison's conception of the classical understanding of politics (*Voyage* 5:277–78). For a more extensive discussion of this, see Chapter 7.

[56] Note that Peuchet's idea that the print media make communication possible in a government over a large territory is presented in 1789, i.e., two years after Madison introduced this notion in *The Federalist*. See particularly *Federalist* 10 and 14.

Central to Peuchet's political thought is the idea of public morality, which is essentially the society's perception of the relationship between duties and interests and its general view of virtue and vice. Public morality is the product of all the local and political circumstances that influence the mores of a people, and it is the foundation for the formation of a common opinion among men. A nation's principles of justice are modeled on those of the generally adopted maxims of morality within the society.[57] For the ancients, Peuchet argued, public morality was identical to the mores, customs, and prejudices of the society. In modern times, public morality provides a "path opened for reason to serve humanity usefully."[58] The advent of the politics of public opinion, and its operation in a large nation, makes charting this new path possible.

In both ancient and modern times, the regime or government (and particularly *la police*,[59] the subject of Peuchet's entry in the *Encyclopédie méthodique*) constitutes the predominant influence on the content of public morality. In modern times, public opinion is the dominant influence on government. The invention of printing and the increased circulation of knowledge in the modern era have fostered communication among men and energetically promoted the formation of a common opinion informed by the views of the enlightened members of society. This opinion guides government, which in turn shapes public morality. As the ideas of the enlightened members of society become "amalgamated with popular ideas," the beliefs and moral habits of the citizenry are purified, ameliorated and civilized.[60] Accordingly, Peuchet argued, public opinion can alter and modify the morality of a nation; it can preserve or scorn the laws. "It is the guide and guardian" of morality.[61] The politics of public opinion makes a peaceful

---

[57] Peuchet, "Discours préliminaire," v.

[58] Ibid., iv.

[59] In *Citizens without Sovereignty: Equality and Sociability in French Thought, 1670–1789* (Princeton, N.J.: Princeton University Press, 1994), Daniel Gordon explains the different meanings attached to the term *police* in sixteenth- through eighteenth-century France. In the sixteenth century the word was essentially a translation of the Greek work *politeia*, or "polity/regime." It meant "the sum of legal and religious customs" that constitute a civilization and act as constitutional checks and limitations on government (19–20). For many writers in the eighteenth century, the term merely connoted the administrative function and competence of government, a reduction in the meaning of polis/police that "outraged the republican Rousseau" (20, 22). While Peuchet's use of the term certainly includes the idea of administrative regulations that establish order in the state, he also captures the breadth of the classical term *politeia* in his lengthy discussion of the importance of beliefs, customs, and opinions in maintaining the stability and health of the political order.

[60] Peuchet, "Discours préliminaire," lxxxi.

[61] Ibid., ix.

revolution in the mores of society possible; it is capable of jarring the virtually stagnant prejudices and established customs of a society. In contrast to the ancient world, public morality in the modern era is not synonymous with custom and prejudice. Rather, in its association with public opinion, public morality censures prejudices and customs and opens a path for reason to shape the ethos of a nation.[62]

The tenets of public morality are refined and humanized in the modern era by a dynamic communicative process that transmits the ideas of the men of letters to the common citizens via the print media. This process of refinement is substantially enhanced in a large nation constituted by distinct levels of governance. Peuchet argued that in contrast to public morality in a small state, public morality in a large nation is much more a "universal sentiment, founded upon the rights of nature and humanity, than a factious opinion or an imitation."[63] Like Turgot, Condorcet, and the physiocrats, Peuchet promoted a multitiered system of representative government. At the local and national levels, discussion and debate can provide the forum for the realization of an enlarged view of interest.[64] Anticipating Tocqueville, Peuchet argued that it is at the local level that one learns how to be a citizen. The practice of suffrage and participation in discussions of the public good may serve to elevate the citizens' views and aggrandize their ideas, perhaps even to inspire a hatred of prejudice and promote a spirit of toleration.[65] They are like so many schools of civic education, where the populace learns to fulfill their duties and to defend their rights as both virtuous men and enlightened citizens.[66] Local governing bodies may even teach people a taste for the pleasures of the mind.[67]

Public discussions at the local level take place within the broader context of a reigning national public opinion. The opinions, mores, customs, and habits of the citizens are altered and elevated both by their engagement with the ideas of the enlightened minds of their time and by their experiences in local self-government. The local assemblies act as forums of civic learning and serve as obstacles to the tyranny of higher governmental authorities; local customs and prejudices are subject to and modified by the judgments of the established opinion of the larger polity. Public opinion is the sum and

[62] Ibid., lxxiv.
[63] Ibid., lxxv.
[64] Ibid., lxiv.
[65] Ibid.
[66] Ibid.
[67] Ibid.

result of this complex and dynamic process of social enlightenment. It is the source of the judgments of the nation, and its power is prodigious. Public opinion "reigns over all the minds," Peuchet argued, and is ultimately the arbiter and guide for the conduct of magistrates and government itself.[68] The "ascendancy of public opinion and enlightenment on the deliberations of government" balance the narrow views of interest and make possible the achievement of public decisions based on the reason of the public.[69] Peuchet ultimately anticipated a progress of enlightenment that would establish over society an "empire of reason."[70]

In opposition to any notion of the progress of enlightenment, whether Condorcet's more optimistic vision that human beings might over time develop a greater faculty of rational choice and actually rely less and less on passion and prejudice, or Peuchet's more restrained view of the possibility of attaching the human passions to a more humane and civilized opinion of right, Gabriel Bonnot de Mably believed that human opinions are too often actuated by powerful passions and interests. He directed the brunt of his criticisms against the physiocrats, particularly La Rivière, and the claim that individual opinions will facilely yield to the rational dictates of *évidence*. Liberty can be safeguarded only in a political system that separates the powers of government and provides counterforces to balance the various passions and interests that motivate men, Mably asserted. Moreover, in large, rich, and powerful nations, there can be no political moderation without the existence of competing corporate ranks in society.[71] These rival orders act to achieve political equilibrium, thus preventing the abuse of power. However, in the clash of these competing claims, Mably also carved out a positive role for public deliberation. He believed that to garner public attention, claimants are compelled at least to assume the "mask of the public good" and show

---

[68] Ibid., ix. Here Peuchet cites Necker's assertion that public opinion "reigns over all the minds" and that even princes must submit to it.

[69] Ibid., lxii–lxiv.

[70] Ibid., viii.

[71] Gabriel Bonnot de Mably, *Des droits et des devoirs du citoyen*, Jean-Loius Lecercle, ed. (Paris: Didier, 1972), 212. Cf. Ira O. Wade, *The Structure and Form of the French Enlightenment*, 2 vols. (Princeton, N.J.: Princeton University Press, 1977), 2:346–51. According to Wade, Mably opposed the physiocrats' view that counterforces and the doctrine of mixed, balanced government were inimical to liberty. Instead, he employed the notion of a balance of power to promote citizenship and achieve the public good in republican government, rejecting the physiocratic notion of enlightened despotism and *évidence*. However, Wade contends that Mably's conclusion "is the important thing," for as Mably declared, "Si ces réflexions sont vraies, vous en conclurez, Mr., que les moeurs méritent la principale attention de la politique, et ques bonnes ou mauvaises elles dédident du sort états" (351).

a minimum degree of concern for the interests of others.[72] The competition of private interests compels "mutual recognition," which induces each individual to "bring the strongest reasons to bear on behalf of his opinions."[73] In this way, public deliberation assists in transforming private interests into the public good.

La Rivière, the comte de Mirabeau (and his father the marquis as well), Turgot, Le Trosne, Condorcet, Peuchet, and the Italian francophile Philip Mazzei vehemently disagreed with Mably's endorsement of a political order based on divided powers, balanced counterforces, and rival corporate orders. Such a system only encourages conflict among men and prevents the society from achieving the stability, unity, and tranquility at the heart of the politics of public opinion. Mably's ideas were as anathema to them as Montesquieu's.

The model of government that Condorcet proposed took its bearing from the equality of rights rather than the identity of corporate claims, narrow interests, and self-serving prerogatives. If Montesquieu had reflected more on the "nature and effects of truly representative constitutions," Condorcet argued, and been less concerned with "how abuses counterbalance abuses," he might have discovered "the means of enveloping them all in the same destruction."[74] The type of balanced government advocated by Montesquieu either destroys itself or depends for its operation on a system of intrigue and corruption. Further, it supposes the existence of two opposing parties, which are contrary to a united and indivisible republic.[75] The unity of the nation is grounded in the authority of the public, Condorcet declared. Indeed, as Turgot had argued, the authority of the public must be collected into "one centre, the nation" – for the nation is the public and vice versa. The exercise of national power must accord with the natural rights of man and the free exercise of his faculties; it cannot legitimately be divided or balanced by vested interests or artificial powers. The logical expression of the united sovereign will, in Condorcet's view, could not be achieved by fracturing that will. He thus rejected all attempts to balance the "vicious powers,"

---

[72] Johnson Kent Wright, *A Classical Republican in Eighteenth-Century France: The Political Thought of Mably* (Stanford, Calif.: Stanford University Press, 1997), 113.

[73] Quoted in ibid., 113; cf. Gabriel Bonnot de Mably, *Doutes proposés aux philosophes économistes, sur l'Ordre naturel et essentiel des sociétés politiques* (The Hague: Durand, 1767), II:205–6.

[74] Keith Michael Baker, *Condorcet: From Natural Philosophy to Social Mathematics* (Chicago: University of Chicago Press, 1975), 260.

[75] *CSW*, 155–56. See also Baker, *Condorcet*, 323.

including the idea of bicameralism.[76] "Man did not put himself into society to be jostled between opposing powers," he wrote, "becoming equally victim of their unity or of their quarrels, but to enjoy all his rights in peace, under the direction of an authority solely instituted to maintain them; an authority which, never having the power to violate these rights, can have no need of being counterbalanced by another power."[77]

Condorcet's praise for the American polity, where "public discussions destroy prejudices and prepare the support of public opinion for the wise views of these newborn laws," is accompanied by a harsh criticism of the machinery of checks and balances in the U.S. Constitution.[78] The American system, he claimed, is laden with a "multitude of springs" and "so many counterweights" that are "supposed in theory to balance one another" but that "combine in reality to weigh upon the people." These are "dangerous political subtleties... too long admired."[79] The comte de Mirabeau, in *Addresse aux Bataves*, followed a similar line of criticism, claiming that Americans had been overly influenced by the system of balanced powers in the English constitution and by the views of the overrated Montesquieu.[80] Peuchet too was critical of the "incoherent system of opposed interests and blind passions" that he thought characterized the newly formed American political system.[81] In fact, he recommended that the new U.S. Constitution be considerably altered.

Despite the doctrine of popular sovereignty that Condorcet advanced, he, like most of the second group of French thinkers, favored preserving the monarchy in France. These thinkers tended to situate the authority of public opinion in monarchical governments and to deny its relevance in despotisms or republics. Moreau viewed popular government as a type of despotism, though he distinguished it from the ordinary kind in which

---

[76] *CSW*, 178.

[77] Baker, *Condorcet*, 265. In 1793, in "On the Principles of the Constitutional Plan Presented to the National Convention," Condorcet wrote, "If the constitution of a people is based on the principle of the balance of the vicious powers combating or combining one with another; if it gives different classes of citizens prerogatives that must balance one another; if it creates permanent bodies and establishes powers long entrusted to the same individuals, no doubt the moment of examining such a constitution will be a moment of alarm because these diverse interests it has created will raise vigorous and implacable war upon each other" (*CSW*, 178).

[78] *CSW*, 79.

[79] *CSW*, 80.

[80] P. F. Willert, *Mirabeau* (London: Macmillan & Co., 1923), 119.

[81] Peuchet, "Discours préliminaire," xxix. Peuchet also commented that in America, public virtue lacks consistency and public morality is not well pronounced.

a "terrible silence" prevails. In popular governments the people are the sovereign rulers; they cannot be checked by any other force, and certainly not by public opinion. Necker and Peuchet argued that public opinion is neither the spirit of obedience that one finds in a despotic government nor the popular opinions that dominate in popular assemblies. It is not enfeebled by the absence of liberty, as in the politics of absolutist systems, nor is it the result of mere self-interest and seething passions that tend to prevail in regimes of excessive liberty, of which Greek democracy is the classic example. Rather, public opinion functions "as a mean between despotism and extreme liberty."[82]

Not all of the major French writers on this question, however, linked the benign politics of public opinion to constitutional monarchies and denied its place in republics. Brissot de Warville claimed that public opinion is more important to republican governments than to monarchical ones. Because of increased publicity in the former, public opinion is of greater relevance to public officials in a republican form of government, and it is a more powerful force in its political life.[83] Brissot himself was a proclaimed republican prior to the Revolution and long before most others of his aristocratic class thought or spoke of any such allegiance. He was a student of the American Revolution and an admirer of the energetic character he saw exhibited by the people of the United States. Not surprisingly, Jefferson became friends with him during his time in France. When Brissot ventured to America in 1788, Madison extended to him an invitation for dinner, which he accepted.[84] Undoubtedly, their conversation that evening turned on matters of mutual interest and concern, among which was likely their shared view of the vital importance and dynamic quality of public opinion

[82] Baker, *Inventing the French Revolution*, 196–97. See Necker, *A Treatise*, I:lvii–ix; Peuchet, "Discours préliminaire," ix–x. According to Baker, "it may have been Montesquieu's characterization of British politics that provided for these later 18th century French thinkers a suggestive context for their analysis of the operation of public opinion. In both despotic nations and free ones, Montesquieu argued, it is generally a matter of indifference whether individuals reason badly or well; in the former, the very act of a people reasoning shakes the foundations of the government, while in the latter, the exercise ensures popular liberty. Presumably then, in a nation that is neither enslaved nor excessively free, the difference between reasoning well or poorly must make a significant difference. Necker's and Peuchet's explications of the politics of public opinion suggest that the concept took shape in this 'intermediate space' suggested by Montesquieu between despotism and excessive liberty." Cf. *SOL* 29:1, 602.

[83] "Discours sur l'humanité des juges dans l'administration de la justice criminelle," in *Bibliothèque philosophique du législateur* (Berlin, 1782–1785), IV:83–124 at 86n–87n.

[84] Jefferson to Madison, May 1, 1788, *PJM* 11:32 and n. 1; Madison to Jefferson, August 10, 1788, *PJM* 11:227; "Memorandum of Books," ca. August 1790, *PJM* 13:288.

in republican governments and, perhaps, the lack of understanding of this among many of their French and American colleagues.

Hamilton's allegations of ties between American republican theory and French Enlightenment thought were not unfounded. Madison's theory of public opinion was not sui generis. He was influenced by the theory of *l'opinion publique* that emerged on the Continent in the latter eighteenth century, and he may have directly borrowed phraseology from some of the French writers. For example, Saint Pierre claimed that a "new empire of reason" was being established, as more and more citizens were being enlightened by public opinion.[85] Condorcet argued that over time, public opinion derives force from the effect of "fixed principles" and unites society under "an empire of reason."[86] Peuchet said that in the modern world Christian morality has united men as brothers; scientific discoveries have led to an increase in communication and the circulation of knowledge among men and have "extended the sovereign empire of reason."[87] The optimism of the French and their wont for the felicitous expression captured Madison's ear and imagination. In words reminiscent of his French brethren, Madison proclaimed: "Let it be the patriotic study of all to erect over the whole [society], one paramount Empire of reason, benevolence and brotherly affection."[88]

Madison shared with the French theorists the understanding that public opinion is the source of stability and authority in a nation. Like them, he learned from Montesquieu and others the importance of public morality in forming the conscience of a nation. Also like them, he associated the nation with the people or the public. Thus, he agreed with many of their criticisms of Montesquieu, especially the condemnation of hereditary and corporate orders in government. He too rejected the design of the British constitution, wherein two major parties are encouraged in their incessant contest for political power; he believed that an amelioration of factions and enlargement of partial interests cannot occur in a party system driven by two major competing economic and social interests. He agreed that there is a distinction between mere will and reason, between ephemeral popular passions and public opinion, and that public opinion should not be equated with the mere will of the majority. Public opinion is not the sum of ephemeral passions and narrow interests; it is not an aggregate of uninformed minds and wills.

[85] See Thomas E. Kaiser, "The Abbé de Saint-Pierre, Public Opinion, and the Reconstitution of the French Monarchy," *The Journal of Modern History* 55:4 (1983), 618–643, particularly 635.

[86] Baker, *Condorcet*, 58.

[87] Peuchet, "Discours préliminaire," viii.

[88] "Consolidation," *PJM* 14:139; emphasis added.

Rather, Madison believed that public opinion results from a process that refines and transforms popular views, sentiments, and interests. His goal, like theirs, was to achieve political rule grounded in the "reason of the . . . public" or "reason of society."[89]

Madison and the French theorists of public opinion shared Rousseau's concern that seductive rhetoric threatens the proper formation of public opinion, but they rejected his view that the proper formation of the general will is harmed by communication with others.[90] They did not think that public opinion draws its moral force from the judgments of the conscience made in splendid isolation.[91] Instead, they believed that communication of the ideas of the literati to ordinary citizens throughout society can inform

---

[89] *Federalist* 49:285; "Universal Peace," *PJM* 14:207; "Spirit of Governments," *PJM* 14:234. See also "Public Opinion," *PJM* 14:170, and "Vices of the Political System of the United States," *PJM* 9:355–57, where public opinion is identified as the *modified* opinion of the sovereign majority. *La raison publique* is a phrase used by Louis-Sébastien Mercier, as well as by others.

[90] See Rousseau, *Social Contract*, II:3, 30–31. Here Rousseau argued: "If the people came to a resolution when adequately informed and without any communication among the citizens, the general will would always result from the great number of slight differences, and the resolution would always be good." When the pluses and minuses of particular wills based on private interests are added together, they cancel each other out, and the general will is "the sum of the differences." Cf. Bernard Manin, "On Legitimacy and Political Deliberation," Elly Stein and Jane Mansbridge, trans., *Political Theory* 15:3 (1987), 345–48. See also Sam Fayyaz's thoughtful discussion of Rousseau's concept of "speechless deliberation" in "Participation without Communication: Rousseau's Conception of Deliberation and Habermas' Challenge," http://www.bsos.umd.edu/gvpt/Theory/Fayyaz.pdf. See, too, Marvin Meyers's comparison of Madison's concept of justice and the general good with Rousseau's concept of the general will and "the sum of the differences." Meyers concludes that Madison followed Rousseau's idea of using private interests (i.e., Rousseau's "the pluses and minuses") to cancel each other out. Nonetheless, he argues, the resulting "sum of the differences" is not sufficient to explain Madison's republican thought; Madison's objective must be understood as "X plus the sum of the differences," which includes such things as "the love of liberty and republican principles for their own sake" (Meyers, *The Mind of the Founder: Sources of Political Thought of James Madison* [Hanover, N.H.: Brandeis University Press, 1981], xxiv–xxxiii). Meyers is correct as far as he goes, but he does not take sufficiently into consideration how the importance of political communication and the genuinely deliberative aspect of Madison's theory sets him at odds with Rousseau. Thus Meyers concedes that "the 'X plus' of my political formula remains a mystery" (xxxi).

[91] The possible exception to this is Condorcet, whose ideas on the issue are not perfectly consistent. See Baker, *Condorcet*, 229–44, 259. Cf. Anthony J. La Vopa, "The Birth of Public Opinion," *Wilson Quarterly* 15 (1991), 46–55. La Vopa's explication of "public opinion" is characterized by the ideal of isolating the individual conscience so that a consensus of disinterested judgments would be formed. La Vopa does not distinguish between this earlier understanding of public opinion and the later strand of French thought on the subject, which not only permits but advances the process of communication and deliberation.

public opinion and elevate public morality, and they were committed to forming an enlightened and active citizenry.

Recognition of the common ground between Madison and the French theorists of public opinion, particularly their mutual rejection of Montesquieu's praise for the British constitution, is, I believe, remarkably helpful in understanding Madison's thoughts on public opinion in the 1790s. It is, however, only a part of the story. Madison clearly worked out the theory of public opinion in his own unique terms, giving it a distinctive republican tone and direction. He disagreed with men such as Necker and Moreau who confined the role of the people to confidence and submission to the government. Although he concurred with the second group of French theorists that the formation of public opinion is a dynamic, interactive process involving the influence of the literati and political leaders on opinion and, in turn, the influence of settled public opinion on government, he vehemently disagreed with the majority of them that republican government is an unfit home for the proper formation of public opinion. In contrast to their monarchical attachments, Madison was a committed republican who envisioned popular government as a *better* environment in which to form and achieve the just authority of public opinion. Unlike those French authors whom he might have termed "theoretic politicians," Madison entertained no Rousseauian illusion that civil egalitarianism would produce a commonality in opinions, passions, and interests. In contrast to Turgot, Condorcet, or the physiocrats, his commitment to the communication and circulation of ideas throughout society was not rooted in faith in *évidence* or the abolition of all "circumstantial and artificial distinctions" among men.[92] Like Mably, he believed that citizens who freely exercise their faculties will naturally form different opinions, be led by different passions, and assume diverse interests. These differences unavoidably lead to the formation of distinct groups or parties in political societies. As much as possible, Madison sought to prevent the existence of parties and to achieve a "general coalition of sentiments."[93] He recognized that this would not always be possible, however, and in these circumstances he advocated making the different parties and interests "checks and balances to each other."[94]

Madison thus rejected the claim by Turgot, Condorcet, and the physiocrats that public opinion cannot form properly or operate effectively in a

---

[92] "A Candid State of Parties," *PJM* 14:371–72.
[93] "Parties," *PJM* 14:197–98; "A Candid State of Parties," *PJM* 14:371–72.
[94] "Parties," *PJM* 14:198; see also "Notes on Government," *PJM* 14:160.

republic or in any society with internal divisions and factions.[95] He believed that he had discovered how republican government could embody a politics of moderation without denying the nature of man. His discovery allowed him to accept, to the extent necessary, factionalism in political life and at the same time to envision how the considered opinion of the community might be fostered, formed, and consolidated. Steering clear of an arithmetic solution to the formation of public opinion, he advanced a prudential approach to political decision making. Accordingly, he acknowledged separation of powers and checks and balances as useful and important prudential devices to control tyranny, and he was critical of those who would dispense with them. In a letter to Madison in 1788, Philip Mazzei, echoing the complaints of his friend Condorcet, disparaged the American system of legislative checks and balances. "In your closet at Paris and with the evils resulting from too much Government all over Europe fully in your view," Madison pointedly responded, "it is natural for you to run into criticisms dictated by an extreme on that side."[96]

Madison accepted that selfish passions and private interests are often motivating forces within the human soul. As a result, he included within his political scheme a place for distributive and mechanical arrangements that would help to control their deleterious effects. He sought, whenever possible, to utilize these "inventions of prudence" to prevent the concentration of power within government and to thwart the power of majority faction. In his view, such counteracting devices do not impede or undermine the sovereign authority of public opinion. Rather, they contribute to the proper formation and legitimate rule of public opinion.

Madison's prudential approach to the politics of public opinion characterizes his recognition that enlightenment is not tantamount to philosophical wisdom, and that in a nation of nonphilosophers a wise government will not

---

[95] According to Keith Michael Baker, the concept of public opinion "implies none of the divisions, factions, passions, or political conflicts of a completely free government.... Public opinion, in other words, implies acceptance of an open, public politics. But, at the same time, it suggests a politics without passions, a politics without factions, a politics without conflicts, a politics without fear. One could even say that it represents a politics without politics" (*Inventing the French Revolution*, 196). Baker's interpretation of the political (or apolitical) milieu is certainly not applicable to Madison's conception of the politics of public opinion, in which the existence of conflicting interests and some degree of party spirit and factious activity are presumed in a free society. Peuchet's rejection of the physiocratic presumption of the force of *évidence* deserves greater attention vis-à-vis this issue; he may well have been less optimistic about overcoming the differences that spring from the nature of man than they.

[96] Madison to Philip Mazzei, October 8, 1788, *PJM* 11:278.

think it superfluous to have the prejudices of the society on its side.[97] His formulation in *Federalist* 49 accepts Montesquieu's, Hume's, and Mably's insight into the difficulty of overcoming the force of passion and interest in the human soul. Nonetheless, Madison sought to meet this challenge and to achieve, to the extent possible, the "reason of the public" anchored in principles of popular sovereignty and natural right. He sought, in a word, to create the nation upon which the French Enlightenment thinkers predicated their theory of public opinion, but which in his judgment they undercut by reaching beyond the realities of human nature. Madison's judicious treatment of politics has much in common with Peuchet's appeal to "healthy logic" in a world that does not admit of human perfectibility; it is an outright rejection of Condorcet's and Mazzei's demand for theoretical purity in public reason. "The Americans are an enlightened & a liberal people, compared with other nations," Madison lectured Mazzei, "but they are not all philosophers."[98]

While Madison's conception of the rule of public reason does not require philosophic wisdom in the populace, it does call for a participatory, enlightened, and responsible citizenry. To accomplish this, Madison argued in favor of a large territory composed of a multiplicity of interests and sects, which would tend to obstruct the force of faction and advance the circumstances that can help foster a common opinion grounded in the rights of nature and directed to the general good. On the importance of territorial size to the theory of public opinion, Madison may have informed and influenced his brethren across the seas.[99] As we shall see, a large territory composed of a multiplicity of interests and sects contributes to the theory of the politics of public opinion by making possible the achievement of an "equilibrium in the interests & passions of the Society."[100] It does so without the need to depend on the British model of institutionalized class conflict or on the French faith in the power of *évidence*.

---

[97] *Federalist* 49:283.
[98] Madison to Philip Mazzei, October 8, 1788, *PJM* 11:278.
[99] For example, in his "Discours préliminaire" Peuchet briefly discusses the effects of the size of a nation on the formation of public morality, arguing that in a larger nation public morality is less likely to be grounded in an artificial or factious opinion and more likely to accord with the principles of justice (lxxv). The date of publication of Peuchet's work is 1789, leaving open the possibility that he was indebted to Madison's *Federalist* essays for this idea. In his 1791 essay "Public Opinion," Madison may, in turn, have been influenced by Peuchet's identification of factious opinion as an artificial or counterfeited opinion. See *PJM* 14:170.
[100] "Notes on Government," *PJM* 14:158.

4

The Commerce of Ideas

In the first term of the Washington administration James Madison had very little time he could call his own. Since he was approaching forty and still a bachelor, this might have been a time devoted to personal considerations and establishing a basis for future domestic happiness. Instead, during this stage of life Madison dedicated himself fully to public affairs and to shaping the future of the new nation. In speeches on the floor of Congress, in public writings, and in private studies, he worked to change the direction in which the Federalists were leading the country. His personal sacrifice was consciously made. He believed that the success of the Federalist program would mean the subversion of republican government in America.

Madison's goal was not merely to resist Federalist views and policy. He also sought to promote a positive alternative to the opposition's philosophy of government, one that, in his view, accorded with the true principles of republicanism. In 1791 he took the lead in promoting the republican cause and providing a philosophic defense of republican principles and policies.[1] Rather than encouraging schemes that mimicked the antirepublican British system of balanced government, increased the power of the national executive at the expense of the local organs of self-government, and diminished the role of the citizenry in shaping public decisions, Madison sought to meet

---

[1] See Madison's "Party Press Essays," identified in *PJM* as "Essays for the *National Gazette*": "Population and Emigration," 14:117–22; "Consolidation," 14:137–39; "Dependent Territories," 17:559–60; "Money," 1:302–10 (in two parts); "Public Opinion," 14:170; "Government," 14:178–79; "Charters," 14:191–92; "Parties," 14:197–98; "British Government," 14:201–2; "Universal Peace," 14:206–9; "Government of the United States," 14:217–19; "Spirit of Governments," 14:233–34; "Republican Distribution of Citizens," 14:244–46; "Fashion," 14:257–59; "Property," 14:266–68; "The Union: Who Are Its Real Friends?" 14:274–75; "A Candid State of Parties," 14:370–72; "Who Are the Best Keepers of the People's Liberties?" 14:426–27.

the age-old problem of placing power and right on the same side and to vindicate the idea of republican self-rule. This challenge was one he wrestled with in the 1780s and continued to think through in the 1790s. He was convinced that the solution depended on modifying the sovereignty in popular government.[2]

The view, so prominent among scholars, that Madison dispensed with the need for civic participation and thwarted communicative activity among the citizenry, thereby undermining popular sovereignty and the democratic principles of the American Revolution, stems from an overconcentration on and an acontextual reading of the 10th *Federalist*.[3] This interpretation also neglects the fact that *Federalist* 10 was not Publius's – or Madison's – last word on communicative activity among the citizenry. In his very next contribution to *The Federalist*, in fact, Madison reversed the tack he took in the 10th essay. In *Federalist* 14 he explicitly discussed how to *encourage* the communication of ideas throughout the large republic. Madison was thus both for and against the activity of political communication, or at least for promoting some kinds of communication and impeding others.

Madison's theory of republicanism involved six major components, each of which was designed to minimize the factious effects of communicative activity and draw forth its didactic potential. These are: the extent of territory, representation, separation of powers and checks and balances, federalism, the influence of the literati on public opinion, and the influence of public opinion on government. Employing an approach to the problem of political communication that combined traditional republican solutions with a new framework of analysis regarding territorial extent and separation of powers, Madison believed he had discovered the way to remedy the vices of popular government and at the same time preserve its spirit and form. This was for him the "great desideratum" that alone could vindicate popular government and make it worthy of adoption by mankind. Madison's remedy depended, as Robert Frost so well understood, on the commerce of ideas and cultivation of the American mind and character.

Madison identified human nature, with its composite of opinion, passion, and interest, as the latent source of factional conflict. When men freely

---

[2] See "Vices of the Political System of the United States," *PJM* 9:357; Madison to Washington, April 16, 1787, *PJM* 9:384; Madison to Jefferson, October 24, 1787, *PJM* 10:214.

[3] See, for example, Charles R. Kesler, ed., *Saving the Revolution: The Federalist Papers and the American Founding* (New York: Free Press, 1987); Lance Banning, *The Sacred Fire of Liberty: James Madison & the Founding of the Federal Republic* (Ithaca, N.Y.: Cornell University Press, 1995), 205–10; James H. Read, *Power versus Liberty: Madison, Hamilton, Wilson, and Jefferson* (Charlottesville: University Press of Virginia, 2000), 181, n. 62.

and coolly exercise their reason on various questions, they naturally form different opinions on some of them. When they are actuated by a common passion, "their opinions, if they are to be so called, will be the same."[4] The problem with opinion, then, is of a specific nature: it is not opinion resulting from the independent operation of the opining faculty that constitutes the root danger. It is opinion actuated and united by passion or interest that gives rise to the problem of faction. When either the impulse that actuates opinion or the opportunity to unite on the basis of such an opinion is lacking, the problem vanishes. Reasoning itself does not create factions, though it may well lead to differences of opinion. Without an accompanying passion or interest to move men to act upon their ideas, such differences are merely philosophic and apolitical. Nonetheless, if human nature is not to be idealized, one must recognize that the impulses toward faction cannot be eradicated; they are as much a part of human nature as the capacity to reason.[5] Moreover, if liberty is to be respected, people must be permitted to form and communicate opinions, even if such views are antithetical to the rights of others or to the common good.

When opinion is easily transmitted and spread, the activity of political communication tends to exacerbate the baneful effects of factious views. This is what generally happens in pure democracies or small republics. Given the ease of communication in a small area with a restricted populace and a limited number of interests and parties, there are few if any obstacles in the path of a factious majority. If a majority of citizens happens to hold a particular interest or passion, given the lack of geographical, occupational, religious,

---

[4] *Federalist* 50:287.

[5] Martin Diamond claims that, like Aristotle, Madison recognized the *"autonomous operation of the opining faculty* . . . [;] but as to what should be done with that capacity, the difference between them . . . is the difference between modernity and antiquity" ("Ethics and Politics: The American Way," in Robert H. Horwitz, ed., *The Moral Foundations of the American Republic*, 3rd ed. [Charlottesville: University Press of Virginia, 1986], 87). I believe that Diamond is correct in recognizing opinion as an independent variable in Madison's analysis, but that he erroneously concludes that, like the variables of passion and interest, opinion is an "independent generating source . . . of factional behavior" (86). Madison is patently clear on the actuating cause of faction in *Federalist* 10: all factions are "actuated by some common impulse of passion, or of interest" (46–47). Passions and interests can attach themselves to opinions (as, for example, "a zeal for different opinions") and, as such, constitute factional behavior, but in itself opinion is not a generating source of faction. In eliding over Madison's meticulous definition and discussion of faction, Diamond can then argue that, like the moderns, Madison believed it is "too risky to rely on refining and improving a society's opinions." Instead, Diamond claims, Madison sought to devitalize political opining about the advantageous and just. In contrast, Aristotle and the classics viewed the refinement and improvement of the citizens' opinions about the advantageous and just as *"the* political task" (88–89).

and other forms of differentiation that would likely characterize the polity, it is relatively easy for the people to discover others who share their view and act together to obtain a common object. This is the case of impulse coinciding with opportunity.[6] The impulse is passion or interest; opportunity is provided by the ease of communication and facile recognition of a shared purpose. When impulse and opportunity intersect, it is futile to rely on other, better motives such as religion, morality, or respect for character.[7] In proportion to the number of people who are known to share the same viewpoint, the greater the confidence a member of the majority has in his own opinion, further increasing the danger posed by an interested majority. "The reason of man, like man himself," Madison wrote in *Federalist* 49, "is timid and cautious when left alone, and acquires firmness and confidence in proportion to the number with which it is associated."[8] Madison's analysis of majoritarian politics is grounded in a psychological analysis of the power of opinion, or what is today called "group dynamics" or "groupthink." The larger the group that shares the same opinion, the more it inspires confidence in others, stymies independent thought and private judgment, discourages checks upon the majority, and removes obstacles in the path toward tyranny. This is the problem that so disturbed Tocqueville about democracy.[9] Madison saw it forty years earlier.

In a civilized society composed of an extensive territory and a large population, the multiplicity of interests and parties that naturally arises in it makes it less likely that a majority will hold the same interest or passion at the same time. In the case where it does, however, Madison claimed that the size of the territory and the number of inhabitants will impede political

[6] See *Federalist* 10:49. For a contrasting view, see Kesler, "*Federalist* 10 and American Republicanism," *Saving the Revolution*, 25–29.

[7] *Federalist* 10:49. See Madison to Jefferson, October 24, 1787, *PJM* 10:213.

[8] *Federalist* 49:283. Cf. Morton White, *Philosophy, The Federalist, and the Constitution* (Oxford: Oxford University Press, 1987), 99, n. 40:248–49. White seems to imply that for Madison (as for Hume) "membership in a group" tends to lead to "objectionable behavior," whether the source be passion, interest, or the attempt "to use reason in arriving at opinions" (248). I would agree that Madison understood the dangers associated with group psychology. However, as I have argued, he did not claim that the attempt to reason and form opinions was an independent generating source of faction or an "objectionable behavior." Cf. David E. Epstein, *The Political Theory of The Federalist* (Chicago: University of Chicago Press, 1984), 68–81; Kesler, *Saving the Revolution*, 25–29. White's conclusion that Publius regarded "true interests and rational motives as weaker than selfish or hostile passions and interests" does not adequately account for his discussion of "public reason" in *Federalist* 49 or of the power of a societal opinion collected and erected on the "principles of justice and the general good" in *Federalist* 51.

[9] Alexis de Tocqueville, *Democracy in America*, J. P. Mayer, ed. (New York: Harper Perennial, 1969), 246–61.

communication. In essence, Madison's theory of the extended republic is a political prescription intended to curtail majority tyranny by a kind of quarantine of factious opinions. If a majority of citizens were to share a common passion or interest at any given time, the challenge of communicating across the extensive territory would make it difficult for them to discover their common motive. The size of the nation has the effect of isolating factions and rendering them unable to spread their communicable disease. In general, effective communication is harder in a large republic than in a small one (or in a pure democracy), whether the opinions communicated are factious or not.

Moreover, the size of the territory presents a tougher challenge to those who are knowingly seeking an unjust or dishonorable objective. "Where there is a consciousness of unjust or dishonorable purposes, communication is always checked by distrust in proportion to the number whose concurrence is necessary."[10] In other words, there is no honor among thieves – and they know it. Madison's insight into the psychology of suspicion is particularly interesting when juxtaposed to his view that men acquire confidence and firmness in their own opinions in proportion to the number of others who are known to concur. But the open communication of ideas depends on the belief that one's motives are pure, or at least not dishonorable. Conversely, communication is guarded when one is knowingly pursuing ends that are shameful or generally thought to be shameful. When a man's own motives are surreptitious, he tends to be distrustful of the motives of others. In a sizable nation in which a great number of people are required to achieve a majority, it is less likely that a majority will communicate and unite for ignominious purposes because the consciousness of dishonorable purposes breeds moral and/or practical hesitancy, and the politics of communication in a large nation amplifies the effects of that hesitancy.

While Madison's proffered solution of the extended territory diminishes the odds that a majority faction will form or unite, it does not forestall the possibility. If Americans lack a consciousness about what constitutes unjust or dishonorable purposes, that is, if there is a lack of enlightened understanding about the principles of justice and honor, then all bets are off.[11]

---

[10] *Federalist* 10:51. Cf. White, *Philosophy, The Federalist, and the Constitution*, 143–44.

[11] This is the problem Madison is virtually silent about in the pages of *The Federalist*, perhaps because it was not the appropriate venue for such a discussion or perhaps because he did not believe that the generation of Americans who fought in the Revolution were in particular need of a civics lesson on the principles of justice or the meaning of honor (though he does proffer a lesson directed at southerners on the unnatural institution of slavery in the 54th essay). Certainly, he continues throughout his life to be concerned about the effect

Under these circumstances, a majority faction would find it less difficult to communicate a common purpose, overriding the obstacle of shame and activating the contagious effect of opinion. Madison discusses a possible counter to this problem of a united, unjust majority in *Federalist 63*, arguing that it is the duty of the Senate in particular to check the overbearing majority's "misguided career." But this is at best a temporary solution, which can only be effective in the long term if "reason, justice, and truth... regain their authority over the public mind."[12]

The principle of representation also helps deny any one group of people a clear, easy path to rule. In a nation with a bicameral congress composed of numerous large legislative districts, communicative activity is partitioned and layered, thereby making it more difficult for a majority faction to secure the requisite votes in the legislature. Moreover, Madison believed that the clash of arguments in public bodies can contribute substantially to the deliberative process and the refinement of the public voice. Nonetheless, he also fully recognized the problem that worried Hamilton: whatever the size of the nation, assemblies are to some degree susceptible to the influence of demagoguery and the heat of capital politics.[13] "The advantage enjoyed by the public bodies in the light struck out by the collision of arguments," Madison said,

is but too often overbalanced by the heat of the proceeding from the same source. Many other sources of involuntary error might be added. It is no reflection on Congs. to admit for one, the united voice of the place, where they may happen to deliberate. Nothing is more contagious than opinion, especially on questions, which being susceptible of very different glosses, beget in the mind a distrust of itself. It is extremely difficult also to avoid confounding the local with the public opinion, and to withhold the respect due to the latter, from the fallacious specimens exhibited by the former.[14]

of the institution of slavery on American character – on what it does to slaves as well as to freemen. He also frets about the future of America when the majority of citizens become landless, turning from agricultural pursuits to manufacturing. See Madison's "Note on his August 7, 1787 Speech in the Federal Convention," ca. 1821, in Marvin Meyers, *The Mind of the Founder: Sources of Political Thought of James Madison* (Hanover, N.H.: Brandeis University Press, 1981), 395–400; Madison, "Speech in the Virginia Constitutional Convention," December 2, 1829, in Meyers, *Mind of the Founder*, 402–8; Madison to William T. Barry, August 4, 1822, in Meyers, *Mind of the Founder*, 343–47.

[12] *Federalist* 63:352.
[13] "Vices of the Political System of the United States," *PJM* 9:354; *Federalist* 58:328–29; "Notes on Government," *PJM* 14:165–66; Madison to Benjamin Rush, March 7, 1790, *PJM* 13:93–94.
[14] Madison to Benjamin Rush, March 7, 1790, *PJM* 13:93–94.

Madison's political realism is reflected in his assessment of what today we call "Beltway politics." Too often the advantages of representation are outweighed by the easy contagion of opinion in a body that meets under one roof in a politically charged city. The heat of capital politics skews independent judgment. This danger is especially acute in members whose mental abilities and/or confidence in themselves are of a weaker nature. The tendency for human beings to distrust their own judgment when they are surrounded by a relatively unified contrary opinion, or to defer making an independent judgment when a common opinion has already formed, results from the infectious power of opinion. In numerous assemblies the danger is particularly great, Madison argued, since they are marked by the confusion and immoderation that accompany the gathering of a multitude. Under such conditions, it is impossible "to secure the benefits of free consultation and discussion ... [for] in all very numerous assemblies, of whatever characters composed, passion never fails to wrest the scepter from reason."[15]

To counteract the dangers inherent in a popular assembly, as well as to guard against governmental tyranny over the people, Madison endorsed the doctrine of separation of powers advocated by Montesquieu, including the limited blending of powers to provide for institutional checks and balances. In *Federalist* 51, however, he reminded his readers that these devices are "auxiliary precautions" and that the "primary control" on the government is "a dependence on the people."[16] Madison would later restate this argument in the Party Press Essay "British Government," arguing that separation of powers and checks and balances are important prudential devices to control the will of the government and protect liberty, but they are secondary to a primary dependence on public opinion.[17]

In the conclusion of the 51st *Federalist*, Madison restated his case for a dependence on the people in even broader terms than he initially had in the essay: the will of the government must be dependent on the will of the society. Accordingly, the public is not only the primary guardian whose watchfulness keeps government within its prescribed boundaries, but also the active agency upon which the movement of government depends. Madison's practical efforts to advance the cause of popular government were based on two equally important theoretical maxims of republicanism: the majority must ultimately rule, and it must have right on its side. In republican government, Madison wrote in a preparatory study for the Constitutional

---

[15] *Federalist* 55:310.
[16] *Federalist* 51:290.
[17] "British Government," *PJM* 14:201; cf. "Government of the United States," *PJM* 14:218.